Basic Aspects of Teaching Physical Education

Edited by

Dr. Rajesh Vaidhya

(B.A. (Hons.), D.P.Ed. (Theory Topper), M.A. (Hindi), M.P.Ed., Ph.D.

H.O.D.

Noida Institute of Education & Technology, Noida (U.P.)

Compiled By

Rachna Jain

PRERNA PRAKASHAN

C-13, Plot No. D-5, Rose Apartment,
Sector-14 Extension, Rohini, Delhi-110085
Ph.: (O) 65749511, 66326118 (M) 9868028838
(R) 27562163. Fax: 23268760
E-mail: lakshaythani@hotmail.com

Published by:

PRERNA PRAKASHAN
C-13, Plot No. D-5, Rose Apartment, Sector-14 Extension,
Rohini, Delhi-110085
Ph. : (O) 65749511, 66326118 (R) 27562163, (M) 9868028838
E-mail: *ektathani@hotmail.com/ lakshaythani@hotmail.com*

I.S.B.N. – 81-89102-52-4

PRINTED IN INDIA 2006

Laser Typeset by:
JAIN MEDIA GRAPHICS,
C-4/95-A, Keshav Puram, Delhi-35. (M) 9911151534, 9350556511

Printed by:
CHAWLA OFFSET PRINTERS, Delhi-110052

Price: Rs. 450/-

PREFACE

The fundamental purpose of the present book entitled ***Basic Aspects of Teaching Physical Education*** is to serve as an introduction to the field of physical education and sports or sport and physical education. It is specially intended for the students of physical education and sports sciences and for the professionals in the field of sports and physical education.

The present book is being planned with a view to enhance the knowledge and skills of professional students of physical education and the public at large on the topics like teaching physical education, content development as a field of study.

The texts in the present study are well-versed and explained in simple English with the view to make understand the professionals as well as the common people about recreational physical education and its scope as a field of study. The book is on the pattern of B.P.Ed., M.P.Ed., D.P.Ed. Syllabus.

Hopefully, the present study will prove very useful for the students and teachers of physical education and sports, sportsperson, as well as for the general readers.

Suggestion on our this book will be highly appreciated.

— Dr. Rajesh Vaidhya
Rachna Jain

CONTENTS

1

REFLECTIVE APPROACH TO STUDENT TEACHING

It is believed by educators that student teaching is one of the most important aspects of the professional preparation of teachers. Those responsible for designing the student-teaching program must remember that the experiences of the student teacher should be a series of activities as nearly like the real teaching situation as possible.

Through many and varied experiences, opportunities should be provided for physical education student teachers to develop the ability: (1) to motivate pupils to develop and maintain good health and physical fitness; (2) to guide learners in the pursuit of knowledge and skills; (3+) to prepare boys and girls to become socially competent and worthwhile citizens; and (4) to prepare pupils to assume their responsibilities in a democratic society. It is generally recognized in the profession that there is great significance in the student-teaching experience as part of teacher preparation.

Student teaching is a basic requirement for state certification and a principle prerequisite for the approval of an institution by the National Council for the

Accreditation of Teacher Education. Student teaching is the time when the student tests the knowledge and techniques he has learned in professional courses in the light of their practicality, feasibility, and effectiveness in a particular situation.

This is the time that the student teacher puts into practice theories of education, along with his own ideas, so that he becomes skilled, and ready for a full-time teaching position. Since it is a time for the student teacher to practice, some educators refer to this experience as practice teaching.

In order for the student-teaching experience to be productive and worthwhile, it is essential to have the cooperation of three people; (1) the supervising teacher, who is a regular teacher of physical education in the school and who has been delegated by the school to supervise the student teacher; (2) the college supervisor, who represents the college or university and assigns and periodically supervises student teachers in schools; and (3) the student teacher, the focal point of both the college supervisor and the supervising teacher.

Purposes

The major purposes of student teaching are to provide: (1) direct opportunities of a varied nature which permit first-hand experiences with pupils; (2) a teaching situation involving problems which the future teacher has an opportunity to analyze; (3) opportunities for the student teacher to put into practice many of the theories studied in various professional preparation courses; and (4) situations where teaching skills and competencies are developed. The objectives of student teaching in physical education in particular are as follows;

1. To provide experiences which will lead the student teacher to recognize, adjust to, and make provisions for individual differences in the skills of pupils.

2. To provide experiences in which the student teacher will work with pupils in many school situations, including the gymnasium, swimming pool, athletic field, and playgrounds.

3. To provide experiences which will develop the student teacher's ability to teach skills and knowledge in a variety of activities.

4. To provide experiences which will enable the student teacher to view the school as a whole and to learn his responsibilities in carrying out administrative policies and in accomplishing the general objectives of the school program.

5. To provide experiences which will give the student teacher an opportunity to work with pupils of all ages.

6. To provide experiences which will stimulate the student teacher's desire for continuous professional and academic growth.

7. To provide expediences that will enable the student teacher to develop into a well-balanced individual, a person possessing a pleasing personality and desirable personal characteristics.

8. To help the student teacher to use the needs, problems, and interests of the pupils as a basis for planning, developing, and evaluating their learning experiences.

9. To provide experiences that will give the student teacher the opportunity to plan units of work and to make daily lesson plans.

10. To provide experiences in which the student teacher learns to select, use, and interpret objective data and records so as to under-stand and guide the populi's growth.

11. To establish within the student teacher the feeling that he belongs to the school and has responsibilities equal to that of a full-time teacher.

12. To provide experiences in which the student teacher learns to evaluate pupils in terms of physical fitness, skills, knowledgeless, and social competence.

13. To provide experiences in which the student teacher learns to develop the ability to handle daily class routines.

What Makes a Good Student Teacher

It is generally agreed that a good physical education student teacher is distinguished by:

1. A sincere interest in teaching as a career.

2. Initiative, interest, and enthusiasm in solving problems.

3. An attitude of inquiry toward everyday situations.

4. A professional and mature attitude toward his work and his colleagues.

5. Thorough preparation and planning for daily teaching responsibilities, including coaching.

6. Willingness to read professional literature in

physical education and in general education.

7. Behavior that is acceptable in his school and community.

8. Acceptable standards of cleanliness and neatness.

Common Terms Used in Student Teaching

Although there are no standard terms in the vocabulary for student teaching, the following terms are generally accepted by educators: Cooperating school. An off-campus school which has appropriate facilities and personnel for professional laboratory experiences, including student tcaching. College supervisor.

A member of the college faculty who has the responsibility for supervising student teachers in cooperation with the supervising teacher in the cooperating school. Professional laboratory experience. All of the school and community activities of the student teacher which involve observation, participation, teaching, and other leadership opportunities leading to a greater under-standing of the teacher's role.

Student teacher.

A college student who has completed the minimum requirements for student teaching and has been assigned to a cooperating school for his professional laboratory experience.

Student teaching.

A period of time when the student teacher, under the guidance of the supervising teacher and college supervisor, teaches pupils in a cooperating school. Supervising teacher. Sometimes refigured to as a cooperating teacher or master teacher in the cooperating school to whom the student teacher is assigned.

The Selection of cooperating Schools

It should now be clear that one of the greatest contributions that a school can make to the future of education is to provide experiences for student teachers.

Close cooperation is essential between the teacher preparation institution and the cooperating schools if these experiences are to be of greatest value, however. The cooperating schools should be carefully selected, since they are the key to a successful student teaching experience. The following criteria should be used in selecting cooperating schools:

Leadership

School administrators and cooperating teachers should be capable of providing the most competent leadership to the student teachers. This means:

1. They are interested in accepting student teachers.

2. They are up-to date.

3. The school's personnel is wholesome and well-adjusted.

4. The school's personnel work cooperatively with the teacher-preparation institution.

5. The supervising teachers have appropriate experience and education.

6. The supervising teachers participate in professional organizations and conferences.

Curriculum

A broad and comprehensive curriculum which provides a wide range of student-teaching experiences in physical education. This means:

1. The school's program includes a wide range of activities.

2. Student teachers have an opportunity to teach at all grade levels.

3. The program of physical education meets the needs, entrees, and abilities of the pupils.

4. Appropriate changes in program are made when research indicates the need for change.

5. Student teachers have opportunities to participate in physical education extra-class activities, all-school activities, and community functions.

Facilities

The school should have adequate facilities, equipment, and supplies for a broad program with many activities. This means:

1. The school's outdoor and indoor physical education facilities permit the development of a comprehensive program.

2. The school allows for sufficient instructional time.

3. It has an adequate number of physical education teaching stations to accommodate the enrolment.

4. It has sufficient and varied enough equipment and supplies to meet the pupils needs.

Getting to Know the School and Community

BASIC ASPECTS OF TEACHING PHYSICAL EDUCATION

It is very important that the student teacher become acquainted with the community in which he will reside and the school in which he will studying the people in the local situation very carefully he can learn things which may directly affect the pupil-teacher relationship in the physical education program.

It is also important that the supervising teacher create opportunities, not only in the teaching station but also in the school and community, for the student teacher to participate in school and community affairs. Often, this requires special planning because special arrangements have to be made.

The supervising teacher has the responsibility for seeing that the student teacher has varied and extensive experiences outside of his regular teaching. By participating in the total school program, the student teacher:

1. Can gain greater insight into the problems and complexities of the day-today operation of today's schools.

2. Will have an opportunity to meet every teacher in the school on a Paterson as well as a professional basis.

3. Will meet and get to understand the problems of other school personnel, such as principals, guidance counselors, and custodians, as they relate to the total school program including physical education.

4. Can meet with other teachers to observe and analyze different methods, techniques, and philosophies in other areas of education.

5. Can develop his own social growth by being diplomatic, a good listener, and capable of expressing one's self.

6. Will become better acquainted with his pupils and other pupils outside of physical education.

7. Will have an opportunity to display a particular talent or skill he may possess.

Many of the values of participation in the total school program can also be attained by participation in community affairs. The student teacher who takes an active part in community activities will develop certain broader benefits to be achieved, including:

1. The opportunity for the student teacher to be accepted and to gain respect in the community.

2. The opportunity to meet some of the parents of the children in his physical education classes.

3. The opportunity for interpreting the physical education program of the school to the community leaders.

4. The opportunity to discuss the needs of the physical education program with members of the community.

5. The opportunity to observe his pupils interact with their parents and other adults in situations outside of the school, which should give the student teacher a better understanding of his pupils.

Roles Played by Personnel in Student Teaching

Student teaching is a learning experience, the value of which depends upon several individuals. Since an increasing number of colleges and universities are sending student teachers off-campus for this experience, it is quite evident that, in addition to the student teacher, the supervising teacher, cooperating school administrator, and college supervisor have significant roles to play. Although the primary responsibility must be the supervising teacher's each of the others must recognize the value of the experience and give their full support to the program.

Without the complete cooperation of these four individuals, this phase of the teacher's preparation would be adversely affected and a less-qualified teacher would enter the profession.

The Role of the College Supervisor

The college supervisor is the liaison between his institution and the cooperating schools. It is also his responsibility to assist the student teacher's preparation in every possible way.

It is hoped that he will develop a close, personal relationship with the student teacher. He represents the college to the cooperating schools and is a key person in building good public relations. It is his responsibility to interpret the college's policy regarding student teaching to the cooperating school. The role and responsibilities of the college supervisor have been stated as follows by the Association for Student Teaching:

(a) Assist the director of student teaching in the assignment of student teachers and recommend reassignment when necessary.

(b) Orient student teachers to the school environment in which they will do their student teaching.

(c) Establish and maintain good relationships between colleges and cooperating schools.

(d) Acquaint cooperating school personnel with the philosophy, objectives, organization, and content of the teacher education program.

(e) Learn the philosophy, objectives, organization, and content of the cooperating school program.

(f) Help supervising teachers and other members of the supervisory team understand and hence improve their performance in their supervisory role in the teacher education program.

(g) Work with college and cooperating school personnel in planning an appropriate program of experiences for student teachers.

(h) Observe and confer with student teachers in order to help them improve their instructional practices through clinical experiences in which the teaching-learning situation and related planing and evaluation activities are examined.

(i) Consult with supervising teachers and other professionals in order to analyze the performance of student teachers and plan experiences that will lead to their greater understanding and, therefore, to the improvement of their teaching.

(j) Counsel with student teachers courses designated to their teaching role.

(k) Conduct seminars or teaching courses designated to supplement and complement student teaching experiences.

(l) Consult with cooperating school personnel on curricular, instructional, and organizational matters when requested.

(m) Analyze and refine their own professional skills.

(n) Cooperate with other college and school personnel in evaluating and refining the teacher education program.

The Role of the Supervising Teacher

The supervising teacher plays two roles when working with a student teacher: he is both a professional teacher of pupils and a teacher's education. All a teacher, his primary, legal responsibility is to teach the pupils in his classes; as an education, his responsibility is to provide an environment which will foster the student-teacher's growth. There is a close relationship between the two roles that the supervising teacher plays, because his legal responsibility will affect the decisions he makes as a teacher's educator.

In his role as an educator, he should provide for the growth of the student teacher by:

1. Orienting the student teacher to the philosophy, policies, personnel, and facilities of the school.

2. Acquainting him with the community, so that he will achieve a better understanding of the pupils in the classes.

3. Arranging his induction so that he is gradually made ready for full-time teaching.

4. Assisting him to understand the pupils.

5. Assisting him to develop instructional skills in

physical education.

6. Familiarizing him with the audiovisual aids used in physical education.

7. Assisting him in the preparation of teaching units, lesson plans, and techniques for evaluating the pupils.

8. Guiding his professional growth.

9. Helping him to develop the ability to evaluate and improve his own performance.

The Role of the Cooperating School Administrator

The key person in the cooperating schools is the school administrator. He is a valuable member of the student-teaching team, and he should assume the following responsibilities:

1. Recommend as supervising teachers members of his faculty who are qualified and willing.

2. Assist in the assignment of student teachers, and coordinate the work of the student teacher and the cooperating physical education teacher.

3. Help in the orientation of the student teacher by explaining the school's policies and procedures, through conferences and materials.

4. Create a positive attitude toward student teaching among his staff and student body, and in the community.

5. Accept the student teacher as a faculty member and give him every opportunity to understand the responsibilities of all teachers.

6. Provide the supervising teacher with free time in which to conduct conferences with the student teacher.

7. Arrange for the student teacher to observe teachers other than the assigned cooperating teacher.

8. Keep the college supervisor informed about changes in teaching staff which might affect the student-teaching program.

9. Work with the college supervisor toward the continuous improvement of the student-teaching experience in physical education.

The Role of the Student Teacher

There are four major phases of they student-teaching experience. Observation gives the student teacher an opportunity to observe individual pupils and to become familiar with class procedures.

It also exposes him to the methods and techniques used by the supervising teacher. Induction gives the student teacher some experience in teaching without assuming full responsibility for teaching a class.

He may be asked by the subdivision teacher to assist in the instruction of individual pupils, the preparation of teaching aids, the demonstration of certain skills, and the evaluation of pupils. Teaching gives the student teacher an opportunity to make use of his professional education, including skills, techniques, and methods of teaching. This phase of the student-teaching experience follows observation and induction.

The starting time for full-time teaching varies with the student teacher, and the decision is made cooperatively by the supervising teacher and the student teacher. Evaluation gives the student teacher an indication of his strengths and weaknesses. Appraisals should be made by the supervising teacher, college supervisor, student teacher, and pupils. The following suggestions should help the student teacher to have a pleasant and beneficial experience:

1. Begin student teaching with a desire to become a successful physical education teacher.

2. Maintain a positive attitude toward teaching during your student-teaching experience.

3. Plan you class activities carefully and well in advance.

4. Develop the ability to cooperate with others.

5. Keep records and reports current.

6. Become familiar with the physical education and general educational policies of the school.

7. Observe the teaching of others in both physical education and other areas.

8. Be prompt for all assignments and meetings.

9. Dress appropriately for the physical education activities to be taught.

10. Make a pleasing personal appearance by dressing properly for the occasion.

11. Accept responsibility for additional assignments to activities related to physical education.

2

LAWS, REGULATIONS AND POLICIES

The program of physical education is of such a nature that teachers and administrators are frequently placed in situations where liability may occur. Therefore, they should be conversant with the law as it relates to their function and they should conduct their program properly, so that negligence can be avoided.

Public education is a function of the state, but the responsibility of educating pupils is that of the local boards of education. Powers given to these representatives of local government are stated in laws state education departments often have established regulations to assist local school districts in carrying out their function of educating pupils.

Although these regulations are not lame they may carry as much authority as law. In addition to state laws and regulations, school districts establish policies to facilitate the administration of their schools. When problems arise between individuals or groups, the matter may be taken to court. It is here that attorneys give their opinions on the legal interpretations, but it is the court that renders the decision.

The decision of the court establishes a precedent

for similar cases that may follow, unless the state legislature passes new or revised laws on the subject.

School District Liability

In American Law, the normal rule of respondent superior is that an employer is liable for the negligence of his employees during the course of their employment. This is not true for most school boards in the United States, however.

The reason lies in our past history. When the United States won its freedom from England, our state and national governments succeeded to the legal status of thc King of England, and "The King can do no wrong."

Today about two centuries later, the rule of governmental immunity still prevails in most of our states. In the performance of its governmental functions, the state, or the school district, cannot be held liable for negligence.

The school board cannot legally purchase liability insurance without statutory authority, because a school board cannot spend public monies to insure itself against a nonexistent liability. Thus, the general rule of governmental immunity protects a school district from liability for negligence in the absence of specific statutes to the contrary.

Because this doctrine has been unfair, however, some states have created statutory exceptions to the rule in one form or another. The three states of New York, New Jersey, and Connecticut have mandatory statutes which say that if teachers are held liable for negligence as a result of an accident connected with their school duties, the school district will save them harmless, or pay the judgment against them.

The states of Wyoming, Oregon, and Massachusetts have permissive laws to the same effect, authorizing but not requiring the states to pay the liability judgment against the teacher.

Legality of Waiver and Permission Slips

A waiver is an agreement in which a person forgoes certain of his rights. When a parent signs a waiver, he can only waive his own right to sue as a parent. He cannot waive the right of the pupil to sue as an individual.

Litigation has sometimes been avoided by parental ignorance of this fact. A permission slip is a document signed by a parent authorizing the pupil to participate in an activity. The only legal value such a form has is that it shows that the school uses reasonable care with pupils and that the parent has received notice of his child's participation in the activity.

Who Pays for Accidents

The education laws of the various states require that all pupils attend school. These same laws, in most states, require that these same pupils take physical education whether they want to or not.

The school provides physical education facilities that the student must use, be they desirable or undesirable. He also is exposed to various pieces of equipment and supplies. The competence of his teacher and the adequacy of supervision cannot be questioned by the pupil.

Suppose the pupil is injured. The question of who is

at fault then arises. Was there negligence on the part of the pupil, the teacher, the school district, or another pupil? There are expenses, the doctor, hospital, nurses, and drugs.

Who pays for all this-the child, the teacher, or the school board? This question is decided in the courts. In almost every aspect of the operation of a school, the educator is recognized as the highly trained expert whose professional know-how gives him the special qualifications to handle school problems. However, when an accident to a pupil is involved, the school, with its administrators and teachers, is not looked upon in the same light.

This is the one time that the school must measure up to the standards of the lay person, to the judgment of the citizens of a community. A liability suit places the teacher and the school district in a court where the decision will be made by a jury of laymen. The question of who is at fault will not be decided by professional educators, but by a jury of citizens.

Requirements for An Action in Negligence

When there is an accident, the plaintiff must allege that there was injury to himself or his property; that the defendant was negligent; and that he, the plaintiff, did not contribute to the injury. In the nature of the relationship, the shoal and its personnel have the legal responsibility of exercising care to prevent injuries to their pupils.

Negligence results when there is a breach of this duty. Negligence is a failure to act as a reasonably prudent person would act under the particular circumstances. Negligence can consist of an omission as well as an action.

If a person fails to do something expected of him by the law, he can be delegant. Also, doing something contrary to what the law expects can be negligence. A reasonably prudent person is a mythical person established by law.

His major characteristic is foresight. If a reasonable man of ordinary prudence should have foreseen the harmful consequences of the behavior, then there is negligence-failure to avoid trouble that reasonable could or should have been foreseen or anticipated. When there is a liability suit, the critical question that is answered is: Should or could the teacher, in the exercise of reasonable prudence and foresight, have anticipated danger ore hurt to a pupil under the particular circumstances? If the answer is yes then the teacher is negligent if he failed to act so as to prevent such foreseeable danger and harm. The specific facts in each case are all-important in determining negligence.

What may be prudent with high-school pupils may not be prudent with elementary grade pupils. The physical education teacher assigned to a playground may be prudent, but the principal who failed to assign enough teachers to the supervision of that playground may have been highly imprudent. Even when negligence exists, there are some cases where there is no liability because of certain legal defenses.

This occurs when the injury was due to the pupil's own contributory negligence and when the injury was due to an act of God.

Defenses Against Negligence

1 Act of God. A condition which is beyond the control of any human being, such as a sudden storm. If prudent action still could have prevented the injury, this is not a defense.

2. Sudden emergency. For example, a physical education teacher, when teaching swimming, rushes to aid one of his pupils who is in danger of drowning. He bumps into one of his other students and injures him. The court may well rule in favor of the teacher, whose immediate objective was the saving of a pupil's life.

3. Contributory negligence by the pupil. When a person participates in certain physical education activities, he access the fact that certain risks are inherent and that accidents may occur despite safeguards and precautions.

Common Areas of Negligence

1. Poor selection of activities. Failure to recognize different degrees of caution to be used in respect to the limitations of pupils due to skill, age and sex.

2. The absence of protective measures. Failure to see the dangers involved in certain situations.

3. Unsafe condition of buildings, grounds, equipment and supplies. Failure to inspect physical education facilities and equipment at regular intervals, allowing pupils to use faulty apparatus or failing to control the pupil's use of areas, equipment, and supplies.

4. Inadequate supervision. Failure to prevent pupils

from taking unreasonable risks.

5. Inadequate control measures. Failure to make necessary corrections, so that the actions of others within or outside a class might create a hazardous situation.

6. Poor judgment. Failure of a teacher to use common sense, so that his actions increase the risks of harm or infra.

7. Undesirable health practices. Failure to administer proper first aid; exceeding the limitations of first aid by giving treatment.

8. Unauthorized transportation. Failure to use a sanctioned means of transportation.

Common Terms Used

Action. The ordinary proceeding in a court of justice by which one person seeks the enforcement or protection or a right, or the redress or prevention of a wrong.

Accident. An event that occurs without one's foresight or expectation.

Defendant. The person being sued or the person against whom court action is brought.

Liability. A condition which gives rise to an obligation and a responsibility to do a particular thing to be enforced by court action.

Negligence. The failure to act as a reasonably prudent person would act under the particular circumstances.

Plaintiff. The person who brings suit for the purpose

of seeking a remedy for an injury to his rights.

Tort. A legal wrong for which damages may be obtained by court action.

Vis major. An act of god, a situation in which the defendant had no control over the accident.

Legal aspects: Situations and analysis

First situation: a crowded Gymnasium

The gymnasium in Jordan High School is only 43 by 74 feet, and it has two basketball courts and six baskets. The second-period physical education class has 60 pupils. Mr. Browning, the physical education teacher, has asked the principal to schedule smaller classes.

Questions

What are adequate facilities? What constitutes inadequate supervision? What are the legal implications?

Analysis

Physical education facilities are considered adequate when they can accommodate all of the activities for all of the pupils on a daily basis, including class instruction, intramural, and interscholastic.

Inadequate supervision is failure to conform to the supervisory standards usually expected of one who is in charge of a group of persons engaged in physical education activities.

Court cases most often involve teachers absentees themselves from a place they are supervising. In cases of litigation involving supervision, the facts are vital.

There are no absolute rules about the number of pupils that should be assigned to a teacher ore supervisor. However, there have been cases of inadequate supervision where one teacher was assigned the sole responsibility for supervising a large number of pupils. The principal of Jordan High School should schedule smaller classes because the gymnasium is inadequate for inadequate for such a large number of pupils.

This was made evident in the court case of a school district with a gymnasium 80 by 43 feet, with eight overlapping basketball courts. All eight courts were used simultaneously. One of the participants was hurt.

The court held this to be negligence because the school should have anticipated injury in so overcrowded a gymnasium when a strenuous game requiring movement was being played.

Second Situation: difficult Gymnastics

At Meridian High School, Mr. Scott, the physical education teacher, teaches a unit in gymnastics. One of the students, Tom Jones, who is obese, is having a difficult time doing very dimple students.

On Tuesday, Mr. Scott has the boys doing a running dive over four boys who are kneeling on the mat. Tom says he can't perform the stunt, but Mr. Scott insists that he try. Tom makes the attempt and breaks his arm.

Questions

Should every pupil be made to perform every activity in a physical education class? What adjustments should the teacher make for individual differences?

Analysis

Every Pupil should not be expected to perform every. Faller to exercise varying degrees of caution as dictated by such factors as age, skill, and sex can be negligence. Teachers should be required to select and conduct activities appropriate to the physical and mental abilities of the participants.

The physical education teacher should know the physical and mental limitations of each pupil, and how they are reflected in performance. The basis for his information is the annual health examination which is most effectively used in school districts where there is close cooperation between the health service personnel and the physical education staff.

THIRD SITUATION: BOXING

Mr. Brown, the physical education teacher at Browntail High School has two boys in his fifth-period class who are misbehaving. He has the two boys stay after school and, as a disciplinary measure, has them box three rounds. Although he gives no instruction in boxing during physical education class, he thinks this is a good way of punishing boys.

Questions

Is boxing a desirable activity to be taught in physical education classes? Is this a desirable means of disciplining pupils? What is adequate instruction in physical education activities?

Analysis

Boxing is not a desirable activity to be taught in physical education classes because the objectives of boxing are contrary to the objectives of physical education. The primary aim of boxing is injury to the opponent. The American Association for Health, Physical Education and Recreation, and the Society of state Directors of Health, Physical Education and Recreation, have both passed resolutions condemning boxing as an undesirable interscholastic athletic activity.

Since boxing is regarded as unsuitable because of the potential danger, boxing should not be taught. Since boxing is not a desirable activity for pupils, it should not be used as a means of discipline. It is questionable whether a teacher should use any physical education activity as a means of discipline.

It such a procedure is followed, the teacher should make sure that adequate instruction has been provided and that practice by the pupils has preceded actual participation in the activity.

In several cases, physical education teachers have been found liable for injuries that occurred to pupils who attempted to do an exercise beyond their skill. In one case, in New York, it was held that the lack of instruction before requiring a pupil to do a somersault may constitute negligence.

Two other cases were boxing and a head-stand exercise. These activities were found inherently dangerous by the courts. Moreover, the evidence showed that the previous instruction had been inadequate and that the pupils had not been warned of the dangers.

Adequate instruction in physical education activities means the teaching of skills through the progression of instruction. There must be adequate time for pupils to practice these skills. The teacher should be a qualified and certified person. Every time a school district finds itself in a lawsuit because of negligence, the first question which must be answered is the competency of the person who had charge of the children at the time the accident happened. If a person holds a teaching license, such license is prima facie evidence of competency.

Defective Playground Equipment

Fourth Situation:

Mr. Jacobs, the supervisor of physical education for the Fairview Public Schools, has the responsibility for seeing that all playground apparatus is in a safe condition. He notices that a 12-Foot slide on the Grant Street Elementary School playground is in need of repair. What action should Mr. Jacobs take?

Questions

What steps should Mr. Jacobs take to repair the slide? Would there be negligence involved if an accident occurred on the slide before the situation was corrected?

Analysis

Since Mr. Jacobs is responsible for seeing that all playground apparatus is in safe condition he should order the removal of the entire slide at once. He should also immediately notify the principal and all teachers at the Grant Street Elementary School that no pupil should be allowed to use the slide in its present, unsafe condition. Prior to the removal of the slide, steps should be taken to make sure that it is impossible for any person to use it. One preventive measure that should be taken is the sealing off of the stairway to the slide by securing boards across the worth of the stairs on front and back. Unless preventive measures are taken, there is probable negligence on the part of the school district and Mr. Jacobs.

There have been court cases where school districts have been held liable for unsafe playground apparatus. In one case, involving a pupil injured on a defective slide on a playground, the school district was held liable. In another case involving a defective slide, the school district was held liable for maintaining unsafe conditions on a playground.

3

SAFETY ASPECTS OF PHYSICAL EDUCATION

Safety is freedom from danger or hazard. Safety entails individual as well as group responsibility and can be achieved only through the continuous efforts of all concerned. Accidents are events that are not foreseen or expected.

They may cause injury, disablement, property damage, loss of time, or even death. When accidents occur, it is quite, likely that someone or something has operated ineffectively. It is essential that maximum precautions be taken to avoid accidents by providing a safe environment for individuals participating in physical education and athletics.

Principles which will contribute significantly to the control of accidents are: (1) recognizing hazards; (2) eliminating or reducing hazards; and (3) avoiding additional hazards.

When proper precautions are taken, the possibility of negligence will not exist and the chance of a lawsuit will be greatly reduced. It is the responsibility of the school administration to develop and organize a school-district safety program. Such a program should involve the efforts of all persons affected and reflect sound principles of organization, supervision, and instruction.

Specific policies concerning administration, curriculum and instruction, facilities, equipment and supplies, first aid and emergency care, and reporting and investigating accidents should be established.

The following policies should serve as guidelines for action.

Curriculum and Instruction

1. Close supervision should be provided whenever students participate in hazardous activities.

2. Teachers and supervisors of physical education should assist students in realizing the hazards involved in various types of activities.

3. In planning the physical education curriculum, activities should be selected which make provision for the given sex, age, ability level, and physical condition of students.

4. Safety instruction in health and physical education should be an integral part of the curriculum.

5. Adequate physical-conditioning programs should be provided so students will be prepared to meet the demands of vigorous physical education activities.

6. Organization for instruction should be related to the facilities, equipment, and supplies available, as well as to the type of activity being taught.

7. Teachers should check equipment, supplies and facilities for possible hazards, and teach students to check.

8. Only teachers qualified to conduct physical education activities should be employed.

9. Physical and mental differences in students should be considered in the selection and teaching of activities.

10. Pupils should not be forced to perform physical activities which they obviously feel incapable of performing.

11. Activities in the curriculum guide should be bases upon the age and abilities of pupils and approved by the board of education.

Facilities

1. Play areas near streets should be fenced.

2. When a hazard in a facility or equipment is identified, it should be corrected immediately or the defective area made inaccessible and its use discontinued until corrective measures have been taken.

3. Activity areas should be level, clean, and free of obstructions.

4. Planning the facilities should be a cooperative effort, involving appropriate school personnel and architects.

5. New facilities should be laid out without hazards, and designed for future expansion.

6. The surfacing of the various activity areas should be appropriate for the activities.

7. Facilities should have proper field or floor markings based on the type of activity and the age levels

of the participants.

8. A color scheme, consistent with recommended safety-color codes, should be used to identify devices and hazardous areas or equipment.

Administration

1. A faculty committee, including student representatives, should be organized to advise on safety problems.

2. All schools should have specific plans for handling all anticipated emergencies.

3. Medical approval should be required for participation in physical education activities following serious illness or injury.

4. Health histories and medical examinations should be required of students before they participate in physical education class instruction, intermural, and inter school athletics.

5. There should be a plan for the periodic inspection of facilities, equipment, supplies, buildings, and grounds as often as necessary to insure a safe program.

6. A detailed plan should exist for handling spectators and crowds at all school activities open to the public.

7. All schools should provide proper insurance protection for students and information concerning coverage should be understood by all concerned.

8. Specific procedures for reporting and investigating cedents should be established for all schools.

9. An extensive school safety program for all schools in the district should provide for safety services, safety education and a safe environment.

10. Advisory services from outside sources such as physicians, attorneys, insurance, and health and safety specialists should be used in formulating and evaluating accident prevention procedures.

Reporting And Investigating Accidents

1. Detailed information should be recorded about all injuries, how ever slight.

2. All schools of a district should participate in a standardized procedure of accident reporting, using a uniform report form.

3. All accident reports should become a part of the student's permanent health record.

4. Accident reports should be analyzed and summarized, and recommendations should be made by the director of physical education to the administration and board of education.

5. All accident reports pertaining to physical education should be examined by the director of physical education and other appropriate personnel.

6. The appropriate administrative officers should be notified immediately of all severe accidents.

First Aid and Emergency Care

1. The staff should be informed about any health condition that might cause an Emergency when the pupil is participating in school activities.

2. Student should receive first-aid instruction appropriate to their learning level.

3. Persons teaching physical education activities should be competent in administering first aid.

4. All members of the faculty should receive formal instruction in first aid and periodic refresher courses as often as necessary to maintain the competence necessary for providing emergency assistance.

5. The school physician should determine medical eligibility to participate in physical education activities.

6. A physician should be in attendance at all interscholastic contests where the activity involves contact. He should be readily available during practice sessions for such activities.

7. The health record of each student should contain information about concoction parents or guardians, as well as the name of the family physician and the preferred hospital.

Equipment and Supplies

1. Selection of equipment and supplies should be based on their contribution to the safety of the participant.

2. Hazardous equipment and supplies such as apparatus, trampolines, and bows and arrows should be properly stored and secured.

3. Equipment and supplies should be adapted to environmental conditions, such as weather, sunlight, and topography.

4. Sufficient area should be provided between

equipment to permit safe usage.

5. Areas adjoining and under playground equipment should have soft, resilient, durable surfaces.

6. Sufficient equipment and supplies should be available for replacing damaged or worn materials that could create hazards for the participants.

7. Protective equipment should be required and used when pupils are participating in appropriate physical education activities.

SAFETY: SITUATIONS AND ANALYSIS

First Situation: Simultaneous Activities

Miss brown, a new physical education teacher at Milford High School, has a class of eighth-grade pupils in a gymnastics unit. She has set up the uneven parallel bars, trampoline, balance beam, and side horse with six girls at each piece of equipment. All of the activities are going on simultaneously.

Questions

How many pieces of apparatus can a physical education teacher adequately supervise? To what extent should pupil-leaders be used in gymnastics? What safety factors should be considered when using apparatus?

Analysis

Miss Brown, being a beginning teacher with limited experience, should not teach with more than one piece of apparatus at a time unless she has assistance from another teacher. More than one nice of apparatus can be used if the pupils have had considerable experience in gymnastics, and if a highly trained pupil-leader is available for each piece of equipment. Carefully inspect the apparatus every day to see that it is in safe condition.

Make sure that the mats are fixed and in proper position. Make sure that apparatus such as the horse and the parallel bars are fixed so that they do not move when mounted. When an advanced stunt is to be performed, make sure that there are mature spotters who are properly positioned.

Stunts should be performed in a series of progressions.

Second Situation: Sneakers

Mrs. Garvey, the physical education teacher in Monticello Elementary School, has several pupils in her primary-grade classes who do not have sneakers. She wants them to participate in the classes, so has asked them to remove their shoes and join the class on the gymnasium floor.

Questions

Should children in the primary grades who do not have sneakers be allowed to participate in activities in the gymnasium when they remove their shoes? Should the teacher insist that all pupils have sneakers when participating? Should shoes with rubber soles be used as a substitute for sneakers?

Analysis

Children who do not wear sneakers should not be allowed to participate in physical education classes in the gymnasium in their socks. Many teachers will ask the children to remove their shoes and paroled negligent.

Negligence exists when a person omits doing something which might prevent an injury. In this case, Mrs. Garvey may be proven negligent because a reasonably prudent person would know that running on the gymnasium floor in socks is dangerous, and she permitted it.

Teacher should insist that all pupils participating in physical education be appropriately dressed, including the wearing of sneakers. The teacher who does not insist has, in essence, omitted doing something which might prevent an injury. Some schools keep extra pairs of senders of assorted sizes which pupils may borrow when they forget their own. Shoes with rubber soles are not an adequate substitute.

Pupils using this type of footwear in the gymnasium seem to have problems with turned ankles.

Moreover, many accidents have occurred in kicking games when shoes have been worn in place of sneakers.

Third Situation: Safe Playground Equipment

Mr. Farley, the physical education teacher at Elm Street Elementary School, has been informed by Mr. Hart, the principal, that the P.T.A. is going to give the school money for some playground apparatus. Mr. Hart wants Mr. Farley to give him a list of apparatus that is considered safe and worthwhile for elementary-grade pupils.

Questions

What are some of the different types of playground apparatus? What is some safe elementary-school playground apparatus? Why should elementary schools purchase playground equipment? What type of surfacing should be underneath playground apparatus?

Analysis

Generally speaking there are three different types of playground apparatus: (1) recreation, such as swings, slides, and teeters; (2) dears; and (3) creative-imaginative, including some recreation and some developmental. Many of the last type take fantastic forms, including animals and trees.

It has been found that most present-day playground apparatus is safe. The one piece of equipment apparatus that has been found to be unsafe is the giant stride (a pole with attached chain and ring). Most schools have either removed it or adjusted it to be used for tether ball. It is natural for elementary-school children to climb and hang. In order to meet this natural urge, elementary schools must provide opportunities for their pupils to use developmental apparatus. Such equipment contributes to physical fitness through the development of strength, endurance, and agility.

Many pupils are interested in using recreational apparatus during their leisure time, and the school should meet the interests of its pupils by providing this type of equipment. Many pupils are interested in using recreational apparatus during their leisure time, and the school should meet the interests of its pupils by providing this type of equipment.

The surfacing under playground apparatus should be a resilient type, such as sawdust, sand, or a mixture of sand and tanbark.

Fourth Situation: an Indoor Relay Race

Mr. Fredericks, the supervisor of physical education, has observed an elementary-classroom teacher teaching her first-grade pupils to run a relay race.

The pupils run to the end of the gymnasium, touch the wall, and return to the starting line. Mr. Fredericks should make several suggestions to this teacher.

Questions

Should gymnasium walls be used for turning points in relay races? What should be used for turning markers in relay races? What safety factors should be considered in conducting relay races?

Analysis

Mr. Fredericks should inform the classroom teacher that the walls of the gymnasium should not be used as turning points during relay races because serious injuries may occur. Many serious accidents have been recorded, even when the walls have been padded. There are many safe turning markers, including Indian clubs, plastic bowling pins, and traffic safety markers.

These should be placed far enough away from the wall so there is no safety hazard. The following safety precautions should be taken when conducting a relay race.

The teacher should explain the rules and directions very carefully.

All pupils should run the same pattern.

All pupils should stay in line and be a safe distance behind the finish line.

All pupils should be wearing sneakers. They should

not be allowed to run wearing just socks.

The gymnasium floor must be free of dirt and debris.

Fifth Situation: Playing Football With a Handicap

The parents of a boy in Summerville High School would like their son, who has only one eye, to play varsity football. The school has a policy that such handicapped pupils cannot play contact sports. The family physician has indicated that it is permissible for the boy to play.

Questions

Should handicapped pupils be allowed to participate in interscholastic sports? Is the school's policy a desirable one? Some handicapped pupils may participate in certain interscholastic sports without permanent damage to their health and well-being.

The physician has to weigh very carefully his decision about whether a pupil should participate in interscholastic sports, especially contact sports, if he has a physical defect. Some athletes with handicaps such as asthma and diabetes have participated in sports for years without any damage to their health.

If a pupil is blind in one eye, however, the hazards are too great to let him participate in sports involving body contact. If the good eye were injured, total blindness might be the end result.

The school's policy is a good one because the chances too great to take.

The personnel should try to get the boy interested in other non-contact fall sports, such as cross-country running. When pupils have handicaps such as one eye, one kidney, or a defective heart, if is probably good school policy to have the medical recommendation of the specialist in each case.

If the school district has a physician, then he should make the final medical decision about whether a handicapped pupil should play interscholastic sports. Since the team represents the school, the school physician should have the final say when there is a difference of medical opinion.

4

PERSONNEL AND SCHEDULING

PERSONNEL

Although facilities, instructional supplies, and equipment are essential to an excellent program of physical education, it is the quality of personnel that determines the effectiveness of the program. The enthusiastic leadership of qualified personnel results in outstanding programs. Leadership, in physical education, means administration, supervision, and instruction.

Supervisory Leadership

One of the responsibilities of the administrator is supervision. In some school districts, the director of physical education assumes responsibility for the supervision of the program, while in other school systems there are separate supervisors who work with the director.

The responsibilities of the director are more comprehensive, involving planning and directing the program. The supervisor is more closely concerned with the operation of the program and the teacher-pupil learning situation. The supervisor should possess the same personal qualifications as other members of the staff.

He should also have adequate successful teaching experience in schools, and one or more years of graduate study. Among other competencies he should be able to observe teachers, analyze their techniques, and evaluate their results. He should possess the ability to improve the teacher-pupil learning situation by constructive criticism.

Administrative Leadership

The individual who is assigned administrative responsibilities in physical education must organize and implement the program on the basis of sound educational principles. He should possess human skills which permit him to communicate successfully and work cooperatively with others. His technical and conceptual skills should contribute to the achievement of both the general and specific objectives of the physical education curriculum. In working with other staff members, the administrator must utilize his leadership ability in such a way that decisions are arrived at by the group through democratic procedures.

Authority and responsibility should be delegated to staff members on the basis of their ability and experience, and they should be directly involved in determining departmental policies and procedures.

Through democratic procedures the administrator develops the competencies of individual staff members and assists them in realizing the goals of the program. Occasionally, however, it will be necessary for the administrator to arrive at a final decision, particularly when the staff is unable to do so.

Classroom Teachers in the Elementary Physical

Education program

Although more and more physical education teachers are being employed by school systems to teach elementary school physical education, there are still many classroom teachers who assume responsibility for this area of the curriculum.

The elementary-classroom teacher in the primary grades of many schools is responsible for conducting the physical education program.

In the intermediate grades there is a more highly specialized program of physical education activities, best taught by a physical education teacher who is more highly trained and skilled in physical education. Even in these grades the classroom teachers play a valuable role by assisting the physical education teacher and by teaching physical education to their classes on the days when the physical education teacher is not present.

Physical Education Teachers

The selection of physical education teachers should be based upon their personal and professional qualifications. They should have the same competence as other members of the faculty and be able to plan a comprehensive curriculum based upon the needs and interests of children.

Physical education teachers should possess the following personal qualifications:

1. Faith in the worth of teaching and leadership
2. Personal concern for the welfare of all people
3. Respect for personality

4. Understanding children, youth, and adults and appreciating their worth as citizens

5. Social understanding and behavior

6. Social understanding and behavior

7. Community-mindedness

8. Interest in and aptitude for teaching and leading

9. Above-average mental ability and common sense

10. Above-average health

11. Voice of good quality and power, intelligently used

12. Effective use of language

13. A sense of humor

14. Energy and enthusiasm sufficient to the requirements of effective leadership.

In addition to these personal qualifications, physical educators should have sufficient professional preparation to insure competency in technical skills and knowledge. Their competencies should include:

1. Appreciation of the place and contribution of our schools in society, including the school in relation to the community

2. Knowledge of the development and organization of our communities and our schools

3. An understanding of child nature and development

4. An understanding of the learning process and

how to expedite it

5. Skill in the adjustment of learning experiences to the nature and needs of people

6. Knowledge and skill in the use of resource materials and of teaching and leadership aids.

7. Skill in the use of appropriate teaching and leadership techniques

8. Proficiency in evaluating the outcomes of learning experiences

9. Skill in making school and community life an experience in democratic living

10. Mastery of basic and related materials involved in the area of leader ship responsibility

11. Knowledge and skill necessary to share in meeting common needs of people, without reference to the nature of the teaching or leadership assignment; for example, health education, physical education, and recreation needs, and guidance and counseling needs

12. Skill in relating learning materials to the total learning experience of the individual

13. Effectiveness in working with others, including pupils, colleagues, parents, and community

14. A point of view in education and recreation that requires that practices be adjusted to all people and their welfare

In-Service Education

In order to produce more effective physical education teachers, develop their leadership ability, create esprit de corps, and guide their efforts toward the achievement of common goals, a continual program of in-service education is of the utmost importance.

A variety of techniques may be employed in the conduct of in-service education. Some of these include graduate study, professional conferences and meetings, workshops, clinics, school visitations, staff meetings, and the reading of new books, professional journals and research reports.

Certification of Teachers

Most state education departments have specific regulations concerning the certification of physical education teachers. Professional preparation, in an accredited institution of higher learning having a teacher-education program in physical education, is usually required.

The purpose of certification for teaching is to assure a school district that the individual is qualified and competent to teach physical education activities. In lawsuits involving negligence, the first question which must be answered is the competence of the person supervising at the time the accident occurred. If the person holds a teaching certificate, such license is prima facie evidence of competence.

SCHEDULING

The utilization of teaching personnel and the scheduling of physical education classes are important administrative responsibilities that involve the total school program. The procedure by which physical education staff and classes are scheduled is indicative of the administrative philosophy of the school and will affect the quality of the program. Scheduling is directly related to the total curriculum and must take into consideration such factors as: (1) the number of teaching stations available; (2) the size of the instructional staff available; and (3) the number of pupils to be scheduled.

Teaching stations. Adequate facilities should be provided in order to implement the curriculum. However, teaching stations, particularly indoors, are usually limited, and this necessitates an adjustment of activities to fit the space available.

In making such adjustments, educational values must be weighed with respect to the objectives of the entire program.

A comprehensive survey should be made of all available facilities before developing a schedule.

Sometimes a classroom may be used, particularly during inclement weather, to teach the knowledge-and-appreciation aspect of physical education. Sometimes facilities in the community, such as bowling alley or skating rink, may be available for use.

Teaching staff. The utilization of the teaching staff should take into consideration such things as their own preferences, their ability to work with specific age groups, and their competencies in teaching various areas of the curriculum. Teachers who possess special skills–teaching body dynamics, games, self-testing activities, rhythms and dance, or aquatics–should be assigned accordingly. This opportunity will usually occur in larger schools, where there are more physical education teachers and a sufficient number and variety of teaching stations.

Teachers who have an interest in younger boys and girls and relate positively with them should be assigned to teach physical education at the elementary level. Teachers who understand and communicate well with older students should teach in the secondary school.

Every attempt should be made to schedule teachers in a manner which makes the best use of their abilities and results in a comprehensive curriculum which best meets the objectives of physical education

Student body. In scheduling students, it is essential to see to it that everyone takes physical education. Students who are well enough to attend school should be assigned to physical education classes.

These assignments, based upon the individual needs of students, will range from total participation to supervised rest. Consideration must be given to the assigning of outstanding students, in order to fulfill their needs, as well as to those boys and girls who have limited ability.

Assignment of the latter group to study hall should not be considered a substitute for physical education. The program should be organized with regard for the student's physical condition and therefore every pupil should have a medical examination.

This should be done prior to his being scheduled for other subjects. In smaller schools, a small number of pupils would be classified for restricted activity, and scheduling a separate class for them would be difficult; in larger school districts the number may be sufficient to justify a separate, adapted class.

TYPES OF SCHEDULING

Traditional scheduling.

Traditional scheduling, involving the same number of periods in each school day, of approximately the same amount of instructional time, has been used by many school administrators to assign pupils to classes. Such a system has not always proved to be successful, however, particularly with respect to physical education.

Modular scheduling.

An innovation which has contributed to scheduling procedures is flexible, or modular, scheduling. This type quire different kinds of time and that students having different abilities should not be kept together in a pattern determined by the format of the school day.

By use of flexible scheduling, the instructional day is divided into a number of time units called modules, rather than periods. By adding one module to another, teachers may assemble their courses according to the time that is required for the specific educational activity planned.

Through the use of computers, flexible scheduling may be established on a semester of yearly basis and can contribute to physical education by promoting greater utilization of facilities, increased student motivation, more efficient staff utilization, and individualized instruction. The physical education staff should make the school administration aware of their departmental goals and of the best type of scheduling to achieve these goals.

The staff should emphasize the specific problems

inherent in scheduling pupils for physical education classes and should stress the rationale of basing the scheduling of classes on the number of teachers available, the number of teaching stations that may be utilized, and the number of students who must be scheduled.

PERSONNEL SITUATIONS AND ANALYSIS

First Situation: Shortage of Coaches

The superintendent of schools has asked Mr. Snider, the director of physical education, to expand the number of interscholastic activities for high-school boys. There are three high-school men physical education teachers, each one of whom is responsible for one sport and assists with another sport, so that each teacher has one free season. Mr. Snider agrees that there should be more interscholastic teams but he also feels that each coach needs a free season.

Questions

How many different teams should one teacher coach? Who should coach the boys high-school interscholastic teams? Should teachers receive additional compensation for coaching?

Analysis

Probably the best arrangement is for a teacher to coach just one sport during the school year. In many small schools, however, if there is going to be a variety of interscholastic teams, it will be necessary for a teacher to coach during more than one sport season.

It is generally agreed that the maximum coaching assignment for any one teacher should be only two sports seasons. Some educators believe that the only teachers who should coach are the physical education teachers; others believe that any teacher should be able to coach. In order for most schools to have a variety of interscholastic teams, it is necessary to use both physical educators and other faculty members. Since coaching is teaching, the teachers who coach should either receive additional funds for their coaching or compensatory time off during the regular school day.

When additional monies are given for coaching, however, the school should have a consistent policy of giving additional monies to teachers who handle the school dramatics, bands, student council, or any other student activity that requires time beyond the regular school day. Since Mr. Snider believes that a coach needs one free sports season, he should ask the superintendent for more physical education teachers or for the assonant of other faculty members who can coach certain sports.

To expand the interscholastic program, it would be necessary to get more teachers who can coach, regardless of whether they are physical educators. If the problem in the past has been to get other teachers to coach, then maybe Mr. Snider should check the school policy about additional compensation for coaching.

Second Situation: Shortage of State

Mr. Browning is a new principal in LeRoy Elementary School, which has 500 pupils. He would like all pupils in grades 1 to 6 have a daily classroom teachers have a free period while their pupils are in physical education. There is only one physical education teacher available for full-time assignment in this school. Mr. Browning realizes that the classroom teachers need one free period daily, but he also realizes the need for all pupils to have a daily period of physical education.

Questions

Should the elementary-classroom teacher have a free period when her class has physical education? Should the elementary classroom teacher have a free period when her class goes to other special subjects, such as music and art? Is it possible to have as daily period of physical education for each pupil and still allow the classroom teacher a free period each day?

Analysis

The elementary classroom teacher is occupied with many additional duties, including lunch room, bus and playground supervision. For her own good physical and mental health, it is necessary for her to have some free time for rest and relaxation during the school day.

Some schools give the elementary-classroom teacher a free period when her pupils are having physical education.

This is unfortunate, because physical education activities offer a unique opportunity for teachers to see children as they really are. Moreover, most elementary classroom teachers are responsible for teaching some physical education even in schools with physical education teachers.

In order to integrate and supplement what the physical education teacher is teaching, the classroom teacher should attend some of the classes taught by the physical educator. This would also be true of such subjects as music and art.

Mr. Browning could make it possible for all of the pupils in his school to have a daily period of physical education by having both the classroom teachers and the physical education teacher responsible for the teaching of physical education teacher responsible for the teaching of physical education. By using the same procedures with both music and art, it would be possible to still give each elementary classroom teacher one free period each day. For example, if the physical educator comes to the school on Monday, Wednesday, and Friday, the classroom teachers could get a free period on Monday and Friday one week, but attend the physical education classes on Wednesday.

The classroom teachers would teach their own physical education on Tuesday and Thursday. Following the same pattern of scheduling for music, art, and any other special subject, would permit the classroom teacher to have at least one free period daily, and would also keep him in touch with what the so-called special teachers were doing. In this manner the whole educational program for pupils can be better coordinated and integrated–and each pupil have a daily period of physical education.

Third situation: Insufficient Staff

The new superintendent of schools in Mineville has informed Mr. Bleecker, the director of physical education, that he wants all pupils in each of the six elementary schools to have a daily period of physical education. Mr. Bleecker is concerned about this request because he has only six physical education teachers assigned to the elementary schools, one in each school.

Questions

What should be the pupil-teacher ratio in order to offer a daily period of physical education to each pupil? What should be the pupil-teaching station ratio in order to offer a daily period of physical education to each pupil? Can the elementary-classroom teacher teach physical education?

Analysis

When the physical education teachers do all the teaching of physical education in the elementary grades, a pupil-teacher ratio of 250 or less pupils per physical education teacher would permit a school to schedule a daily period of physical education for each pupil.

In order to have a daily period of physical education in the indoors teaching station, it is necessary to have approximately one teaching station for each 250 pupils.

Since each school in Mineville has approximately 500 pupils, each school would need two indoors teaching stations. A teaching station indoors may be such areas as the gymnasium, swimming pool, playroom, and classroom.

In most states the elementary-classroom teacher is certified to teach elementary physical education. Often, however, because of a lack of interest and background, the elementary classroom teacher is not well qualified to teach elementary physical education. Mr. Bleecker should ask the superintendent of schools for six more physical education teachers. A total of twelve physical education teachers in the six schools would allow each child to have a daily period of physical education. If he is unsuccessful in obtaining these additional teachers, he should have the superintendent of schools ask the elementary-school principals to have their classroom teachers supplement the physical education teaching.

Fourth Situation Shortage of Teachers for Girls

There is a shortage of women physical education teachers, and it is impossible for Mr. Duncan, the principal at Ridgeway High School, to employ one for the high-school girls's classes. He has received applications from three men physical education teachers and two women teachers who are not certified in physical education.

Questions

Who should teach physical education to high-school girls? What are some of the difficulties when men teach physical education to high-school girls? What are some of the problems when an uncertainty woman teacher teaches physical education to high-school girls?

Analysis

The person best qualified to teach physical education to high-school girls is the women physical education teacher. She has a background also appreciates and recognizes the differences in their anatomical, physiological, and emotional characteristics.

The female physical education teacher is able to supervise the girls dressing room and showering room. A woman physical education teacher can discuss freely the health problems of high-school girls.

When men teach physical education to high-school girls, the program is often basically a boys activities program with boys rules. It is impossible for the man to supervise the girls in the dressing room and showers, and girls do not feel free to discuss their health problems freely with men.

An uncertified women teacher may lack the background to teach an adequate program, however. If she does not know proper spotting techniques, some pupil may be injured. Many uncertified female teachers can teach skills in only a few activities, and consequently the program is quite limited.

There is no reason why a man must always teach boys. If a man can teach girls in a coeducational class, he should be able to tcach girls in a girls in a coeducational class, he should be able to teach girls in a girls class. Since Mr. Duncan has applications from three certified male physical education teachers, he should hire the man he thinks is the best teacher, rather than an uncertified female teacher.

Fifth Situation: Supervision of Intramural Activities

The principals in the three elementary schools of Eariville are concerned because the three new physical education teachers go to Eariville High School after their last classes to assist in coaching varsity teams. Consequently, there are no intramural activities after school for the intermediate-grade boys and girls.

Question

Should the elementary physical education teacher be responsible form the intramural activities for the elementary-grade pupils? Should the elementary physical education teacher be allowed to coach the interscholastic teams at the high school?

Analysis

The elementary physical education teacher should be responsible for the intramural activities for the elementary-grade pupils, since this is an integral part of the physical education program. If these intramural activities are not offered to the intermediate-grade pupils, their physical education program is not a complete one. In small school districts where it is a problem to get sufficient staff to coach the boys, varsity high-school teams the elementary physical education teacher is often asked to coach.

If he is willing to coach and if it does not interfere with his prior responsibility to handle the elementary-grade intramural activities, this may be a satisfactory arrangement. This can be managed by having the elementary physical education teacher supervise the intramural activities directly after school.

When he is through with this part of the program, he can go to the high school to coach. This arrangement works well in school districts where the elementary school day ends earlier than the secondary school, or in school districts where varsity teams practice at a later hour or after dinner. It must be kept in mind, however, that there is a limit to the physical stamina of a teacher.

5

FACILITIES

The personnel responsible for the organization, administration and conduct of the physical education program has an important role in the development of functional facilities that are adequate for the program.

These facilities should be based on: (1) the physical education activities, which are designed to meet the interests and needs of the pupils: (2) the amount of time that the pupils spend in class instruction, intramural, extramurally, and interscholastics; (3) the ultimate enrollment of the school; and (4) the official size of playing areas. The facilities should be planned so that they are functional and take into consideration the various needs for organized recreation.

Such planning would provide facilities for both physical education and recreational programs and would spread the cost of this part of the modern school plant. The use of the elementary school as a neighborhood center and the secondary school as a community center has saved the cost of constructing separate recreation centers in many communities.

INDOOR FACILITIES

In planning the indoor facilities with which to administer and carry on the physical education program, basic consideration should be given to the following areas: gymnasium, swimming pool, apparatus storage room, boys, dressing room and showering rooms, girls, dressing room and showering rooms, adapted activities room, physical education office, team room, equipment-drying room, laundry room, supply storage room, and classroom.

Gymnasium

The gymnasium should be at or slightly above ground level. The auxiliary facilities, when possible, should be adjacent and at the same level. This unit should be readily accessible from the rest of the building and from the outdoor physical education facilities.

The facilities should be near the auditorium and cafeteria in order that they may be used in conjunction with community recreational activities without opening the entire building.

Gymnasium Floor Space.

It will be necessary to provide, within the floor space, as many separate class areas as are needed for the simultaneous activities of different physical education classes, and of a size which will accommodate a maximum-size class of 40 pupils.

In addition to these areas there should be a reasonable amount of seating space for spectators when the physical education areas are used for interscholastic sports. In elementary schools requiring a single teaching station, the minimum floor space should be 40 by 60 feet, or one space 60 by 80 feet which is divisible by a folding partition. If it is anticipated that the school will serve as a neighborhood deuteration center, a larger area should be provided to accommodate such activities as basketball, badminton and volleyball. In secondary schools where the program and enrollment require only a single teaching station, a minimum floor space 52 to 84 feet should be planned.

An area 84 by 104 feet of clear floor space, exclusive of folded-back bleachers, will give two teaching stations of sufficient size. It should be equipped with a motor-driven folding partition which is soundproof and extends from floor to ceiling.

Curtains and nets in place of the partition are inadequate and not desirable. The folding bleachers will provide substantial seating capacity for spectator sports in a minimum of additional space, as compared with fixed seating.

When the program and enrollment of the school require more than two teaching areas, the additional facilities may be secured by extending the gymnasium area to provide another teaching station or by adding small group-activity rooms.

An additional teaching station may be gained by constructing a swimming pool. A reasonable pool size, and one which will accommodate interscholastic swimming competition, is 42 by 75 feet 1 inch in length.

Gymnasium Treatment

The finish of the gymnasium should be in keeping with the purpose of the room. There is no need for elaborate appointments. The room should be simple. It must lend itself to hard, vigorous usage. The walls should be light in color, and smooth and regular, with no projections or sharp corners that may be hazardous to pupils. Care should be taken to insure that doors and doorways are not so located as to be a safety hazard. For example, doors in the center of the end walls of the gamma sum are a hazard to those using the gymnasium for active games as well as to those passing in the corridor on the opposite side of the doors.

Corner locations are preferable. Acoustical treatment is imperative. The height of the gymnasium proper should never be less than 18 feet; and a maximum of 20 to 22 feet is preferable.

If beams are left exposed, equipment can be suspended. If the ceiling is to be furred below the structural members, the attachment of suspended equipment should be planned and eyebolts provided during the construction of the room. Some schools have found that eyebolts provided in each corner of the gymnasium during the construction of the room. Some schools have found that eyebolts provided in each corner of the gymnasium during its construction have proven useful when decorating the room for school social events. When equipment which will require fastening to the wall or floor, such as horizontal bars and volleyball standards is to be used, a layout of its placement should be made so that wall boards and floor sockets can be provided at the time of construction.

When the design of the building will permit, high bilateral lighting is desirable. In order that the gymnasium wall may be used for rebounding in such activities as handball, fielding a softball, and handling a basketball, window sills should be placed 10 feet above the floor. If possible, they should be arranged so that pupils using the basketball buckboards in the daytime are not looking up into the windows. If this arrangement is not possible, they should be provided with some type of shade or constructed of diffusing glass to eliminate glare. Windows divided into small panes of heavy plate or tempered plate glass are desirable, as window guards are not then needed.

The elimination of guards makes it easier to open the windows. The generally preferred flooring for the gymnasium is first-quality, norther, hard-strip maple, laid on sleepers. It makes a floor that is resilient, durable, smooth, and easily cleaned. The floor should always be designed so that it can be ventilated underneath to prevent dry rot. Experience has proved that the gymnasium floor should never be located below grade level. A finish especially designed for gymnasiums should be used rather than ordinary floor finishes or varnishes.

Floor markings should be worked out according to the games and activities to be played. The lines should be painted on the gymnasium floor in differentiating colors and varying widths before the final finish is applied. A minimum of 3 feet should be allowed for a safety zone between the adjacent lines of the playing areas and between the lines of the playing areas and the walls of the gymnasium. A suggested scheme of colors and width of lines is:

Badminton	—Red	–1 1/2 inches wide
Basketball	—Black	–2 inches wide
Shuffleboard	—Yellow	–1 1/2 inches wide
Volleyball	—Green	–2 inches wide

Indoor Baseball —Blue –2 inches wide

Circle Games —Orange–2 inches wide

Drinking fountains should be located in the corridors, convenient to the doors leading from the gymnasium. A safety hazard is involved in placing fountains in the gymnasium because of the inevitable sloshing of water. The number, size and details of exit doors should meet the current Building Exit Code of the National Fire Protection Association.

Teaching Stations

A teaching station is defined as a room that can be regularly scheduled for a class under the direction of a teacher. Wise planning establishes some priority for the types of teaching stations. For the school which needs three stations, it would be wise to give first priority to a gymnasium with a folding partition and two stations, and second priority to a pool as the third station. The next priority, if a swimming pool is not possible, is a single teaching station.

The number of teaching stations needed for a school will depend upon:

1. The ultimate enrollment of the school.

2. The number of pupils in a physical education class.

3. The number of periods a teaching station is scheduled for use per week.

3. The number of periods each pupil is scheduled for physical education per wheel.

4. The number of activities and pupils in the extra-class program.

The Small Group-Activity Room and Auxiliary Gymnasium

These rooms will accommodate apparatus, stunts and tumbling, wrestling, adapted activities and rhythms and dance. The size of the groups, however, will be limited. In elementary schools these rooms should be at least 36 by 52 feet, with a minimum height of 12 feet. In secondary schools, they should be at least 40 by 60 feet, with a minimum height of 14 feet.

Bulletin Boards.

Bulletin boards should be provided and placed in a well lit area near the dressing rooms and showering rooms where they may readily be seen by all pupils. Glass-covered boards make for a neat appearance and protect the boards from being defaced.

Electrical Installation

Provision should be made for the installation of a separate public-address system, picture projectors, radio, television, record players, cleaning machines, and electric scorpaenids. The controls for the gymnasium lighting should be conveniently located, recessed, and keyed.

Swimming Pool

The swimming pool should be planned and constructed in accordance with the desires and needs of the school and community it is to serve. Since swimming is an integral part of the physical education program, the pool site should be integrated with the other physical education facilities. Building costs can be saved by having such facilities as the lockers, showers, toilets, and drying rooms that service the regular physical education classes also be used by the swimming groups, although in large schools there may be merit in having swimming pools with their own dressing and showering facilities.

In elementary schools, an instructional pool of 3 to 4 feet of constant depth, 30 feet in width, and 60 feet in length will save considerable cost. The slope of the bottom of the pool should be governed by the purposes for which it will be used. The slope will determine how much of the pool can be used for instructional purposes and how much will be available for safe diving. For safety, the slope should be a maximum of 1 foot for every 15 feet. Approximately 60 per cent of the pool area should be shallow water in order to provide enough area to teach beginning swimmers.

When the program includes lifesaving, synchronized swimming, and other deep water skills, 40 per cent of the pool area should be deeper water.

There should be adequate floor space around the pool for a deck area.

This serves as a place for rest periods and for the conduct of land drills and demonstrations. The surface in this area should be non-slip, and deck drains should be properly spaced throughout.

All pool markings should be imbedded in the building materials so that they are permanent. The lane markings on the bottom of the pool should be of a dark color and designed according to regulations governing swimming competition.

The number and height of the diving boards will be determined by the size of the pool, the depth of the water, and the height of the ceiling. Recessed ladders should be located at the corners of the pool, with handrails.

There should be an office with a vision panel or a small glass enclosed cubicle adjacent to the pool deck. It should have a clear, unobstructed view of the entire swimming area.

Here such things as teaching materials, record player, and personal belongings may be housed. As an indispensable safety measure, this office or cubicle should have a telephone for direct outside calls.

Laundry Room

The laundry room should be of sufficient size to accommodate the equipment. It is much better to have the commercial rater than the home type, including the washer and dryer. In addition to towels, physical education uniforms can be washed, including many items of clothing used in interscholastic activities that are frequently sent out to be dry cleaned. Laundry from other areas, such as the cafeteria, can also be washed in this room.

Dressing Room and Showering Room

Since dressing and showering are recognized as integral parts of the health and physical education programs, it is desirable that pupils in the elementary schools have an opportunity to dress and shower during the physical education class and extra-class program. There should be separate rooms for boys and girls so that they can be used simultaneously during coeducational activities.

Eight to twelve year old pupils are ready for showering and should not be denied the opportunity of establishing this desirable health practice. The health and safety of pupils should be a primary concern of the school, and provision should be made for third and fourth-grade pupils these grades there are usually fewer problems with this part of the program in junior and senior-high school.

Boys Dressing Room and Showers

The location and size of the boys dressing room and showers, and the arrangement of the facilities within the rooms, are of great importance in the administration of the physical education program of the school.

The preferred location is on the same floor as the gymnasium and adjacent to it, so that pupils can pass directly to and from the gymnasium without going into the corridors of the school. It is also desirable that pupils be able to pass directly between the dressing room and the outside playing fields without using the general school corridors. It should also be possible to enter the dressing room from the corridor without going into the gymnasium. If a team room is provided, it should be possible to enter it directly from the playing field.

Lockers should be of two types, the gymnasium suit or storage locker and the street clothes or dressing lower. For hygienic reasons a storage locker 9 by 12 by 24 inches, or 9 by 12 by 30 inches is preferred to the box-type locker of this length it is possible to hang up the physical education uniform and thereby insure drying and ventilation. A dressing locker 12 by 12 by 60 inches or 12 by 12 by 72 inches, is satisfactory.

One storage locker must be provided for each boy using the dressing room, and one dressing locker is required for each boy in the maximum size physical education class. In addition, there should be a sufficient number of dressing lockers to hold the uniforms of the largest squad in the various interscholastic sports in which the school competes.

These lockers may be housed in a space set aside for them in the dressing room or in a separate team room adjacent to the body-drying space. When a team room is provided, a small section of it may be partitioned off to serve as a drying room for the uniforms. This room should have positive ventilation and sufficient heat to insure drying.

The dressing lockers used by the physical education classes should be interspersed equally among the rows of storage lockers. The rows of lockers should not be closer than 5 feet face to face. All lockers should be mounted on a cove masonry base. The locker arrangement within the room should be such as to facilitate the supervision of all activity therein from the physical education office through a glass panel provided for that purpose.

Another type of storage is handled through a basket system. Several types have been used successfully, such as the post-office basket, basket storage on movable trucks, and attendant-operated.

Fixed benches should be provided. Mirrors should be conveniently located in several places around the dressing room. A drinking fountain should be installed.

If the dressing facilities are to be used by adults, the only additional requirement is that each adult be provided with a storage locker.

In order to determine the area needed for the dressing room, it is necessary to know the following facts: (1) the total number of different pupils who will be using the dressing room; (2) the number of storage lockers in each unit of the battery arrangement; (3) the peak-load of pupils using the dressing room at one time; and (4) the area required for each battery of lockers.

The showering room may have either the wall-type group shower arrangement or the walk-around arrangement. In either case there must be enough shower heads to accommodate the largest physical education class that will result from the school's enrollment. One vandalproof shower head should be planned for each four boys in the class if the group-shower arrangement is used and one for each three boys if the walk-around arrangement is used. Shower heads should be at least 4 feet apart and not more than 5 feet above the floor in secondary schools. Elementary-school showers should be between 48 and 54 inches from the floor.

In large showering rooms having the group-shower arrangement, better use can be made of the center area by having a dwarf-type central wall, 5 to 6 feet high, with shower heads on both sides.

A control for the water supply should be placed outside of the shower room where it may be operated by the teacher.

Where group shower is used, at least one shower head should be equipped for independent control. The remainder of the shower heads should be adjusted so that the temperature of the water will vary from warm to tepid to cool. The water temperature should never exceed 110^0 F.

A liquid-soap dispenser outlet may be located at each shower head in the group shower. About three soap outlets should be distributed along the in side of the walk-around shower and at least two at the turn before starting down the out side. These soap outlets should be supplied from a central reservoir of sufficient size to accommodate a day's supply of soap.

Them floor and walls of the showering room should be constructed of an impervious material. The material used for the floor should be abrasive or nonskid as well.

The ceiling and walls should be left unpainted. Sufficient drains should be provided, and so located that no pupil need stand in or walk through waste water.

The body-drying space is an essential adjunct to the showering space. It should be so located that the pupils must pass through it after showering, before they enter the dressing room proper.

It should be large enough to accommodate as many pupils as will be in the shower at one time. Ordinarily, 150 to 200 square feet of floor space will be adequate. Towel service is desirable and is found in more and more schools. When towel service is to be offered, a towel distribution cubicle with a window opening into the body-drying space should be provided. Sufficient hooks for hanging up towels should be provided around the wall of the body-drying space.

A hamper or used-towel receptacle is needed at or near the opening between the body-drying space and the dressing room.

The wall between the drying room and the dressing room may be of the dwarf type, 4 to 6 feet high. The opening between the body-drying space and the dressing space should be at least 4 feet wide, to permit pupils to pass each other. The opening between the body-drying space and the shower space should be of like width and should contain a sill 6 inches high, to prevent water on the floor of the shower space from running into the body-drying space. Drains should be located in the body-drying space so that water dripping from the body will be carried away and not tracked into the dressing room.

Girls Dressing Room and Showering Rooms.

Everything that has been said concerning the dressing, showering, and drying space for boys may be repeated for the facilities for girls.

In order to meet the concern of some parents about girls using group showers, there should also be one or two individual shower and dressing-booth cubicles, according to the size of the school. However, most of the showers should be of the group type because they are less expensive to install, easier to supervise, and easier to keep clean. Shower heads should be located not more than 4 feet, 6 inches from the floor. Several mirrors should be provided so the girls can complete their grooming.

Toilets.

Toilets should always be located in the dressing

room prober, not in the body-drying space. It should not be necessary for pupils to enter either the body-drying space or shower space except when undressed for the shower. There should be a minimum of two water closets and one lavatory in girls dressing room for a class of 40 pupils. In the boys dressing room there should be a minimum of one water closet, one urinal, and one lavatory for a class of 40 pupils.

The lighting of the showers and the body-drying and dressing rooms should be so minimum of 5 foot-candles and the switch for the lights of the showers and body-drying space should be located in the dressing room. The rooms should be positively ventilated, and heated to 78^0 F.

Team dressing Room

In the senior high school it is desirable to have a separate home-team dressing room for boys on the interscholastic squads. This room should contain full-length lockers. In order to ascertain the area needed for this room it is necessary to know the following facts: (1) the total number of different pupils that will be using the team; (2) the area required for each locker; and (3) the peak load of pupils using the team room at one time.

Equipment Drying Room

The drying room for equipment should be adjacent to the team room. It should be of sufficient size to take care of the peak load of equipment to be dried at one time. There should be sufficient circulation of air at a high temperature, in order to insure proper drying of the equipment.

Physical Education Offices

There should be separate offices for men and women physical education teachers. If offices are provided for individual teachers, there should be 100 to 130 square feet of space; when group offices are needed, there should be 70 to 90 square feet of space for each teacher. In large schools, consideration should be given to having group offices for the several teachers and a separate office for the chairman or department head. There should be enough room for desks and files, and limited cabinet space for the storage of some instructional supplies, such as basketballs, footballs, baseballs, volleyballs, bats, and tennis rackets. There should be some dressing lockers for physical education teachers, other teachers who are coaching, and athletic officials.

Separate showers and toilet facilities for the teachers are desirable. These rooms should be adequately lighted, heated, and ventilated. The physical education offices should be proximate to the gymnasium and the dressing room, and should enter upon both of these rooms.

Vision panels between the offices and the dressing rooms and showering rooms, and also between the offices and the indoor teaching stations, are desirable because they provide additional safety and supervision of classes when the teacher is called to his office.

Classroom

It is desirable to have available at least one regular classroom equipped with the usual teaching aids as well as for the use of audiovisual materials. This room is a desirable area to teach the knowledge-and-appreciation aspects of physical education. The utilization of such a room saves valuable instructional time in the gymnasium and on the playing fields.

Apparatus and Supply Storage

Good design of the apparatus and supply storage room will ensure that it has three essential characteristics: easy access from the gymnasium floor; door openings wide enough to permit the moving of equipment from the gymnasium floor into the storage space with ease; and enough space to accommodate all the movable equipment.

Preferably, the apparatus and supply storage room should be adjacent to the gymnasium. When it is necessary to locate the apparatus storage room across a corridor from the gymnasium, care should be taken that the doors of the two rooms are directly opposite. Six-foot doors with a flush threshold are needed to permit the movement of equipment from the gymnasium to the storage space.

Consideration should be given to having an overhead door, so that when the room is being used the is neither an obstacle not a hazard.

The usual apparatus and supplies requiring storage space include parallel bars, horse, buck, springboard, beat board, volleyball standards and nets, horizontal bars, stall bar benches, mats, testing equipment, archery targets, out-of season uniforms and equipment, and so on. A ray schools. A room with 200 to 225 square feet of floor space should provide sufficient storage space for elementary schools.

The apparatus and supply storage room should be well lighted and should have positive ventilation. It should be equipped with cabinets and bins in which those articles of supplies that are in daily use, such as volleyballs, basketballs, indoor baseballs, and bats, may be kept. These facilities should be provided with locks. Provision should also be made for storing equipment and supplies which have not been put into use. Built-in-shelves are generally recommended for this type of storage.

OUTDOOR FACILITIES

In planning the outdoor facilities to serve the pupils in a school, it should be kept in mind that the modern school has two major needs: (1) to provide the physical education facilities that will permit the program to meet the needs and interests of all pupils during the school day; and (2) to provide the physical education and recreation facilities that meet the needs and interests of all pupils participating in activities after school hours. Such planning is sound because it provides for maximum utilization of all facilities and allows for professional supervision and economical operation.

The outdoor physical education and recreation areas should be planned according to the program offered and the number of pupils to be served during the periods of peak or maximum load. The program, since it is based on the pupils needs and interests, is of primary importance. Regardless of the number of pupils to be served, the program dictates the necessity of having certain areas of more or less definite size.

The National Facilities Conference on Planning

Areas and Facilities for Health, Physical Education, and Recreation proposes standards which should be useful in getting functionally planned and more adequate facilities for neighborhoods and communities. The park-school is a school building on a park site which is designed to function as a center for programs of education and recreation throughout the year. The standards recommended for park-schools are as follows:

1. Neighborhood Park-School. This type of educational recreation center should be a combination of and elementary school and a neighborhood park. These areas and facilities should be planned for dual use of education and recreation for the people living in a neighborhood. The recommended minimum area for a neighbourhood park-school is 20 acres.

2. Community Park-School. This type of educational-recreation center should be a combination of a junior high school and community park. These areas and families should be planned for dual use of education and recreation for people living in the community. The recommended minimum area for a community park-school is 35 acres.

3. Community Park School. This type of area and facility is planned for the youth and adults in a community to meet a wide range of educational and recreational needs and interests in a community. It is usually referred to as a combination of a community park-school is 50 acres.

Elementary School

The program of physical education planned for the different age groups in the elementary grades should include certain basic activities that need specific facilities. Children in kindergarten and the first two grades engage in such activities as climbing, hanging, and jumping. Many of their activities should provide for much freedom of movement and the development of the large muscles. The program for the third and fourth grades should include running, jumping, kicking, throwing, and catching. The program for the fifth and sixth grades should place a greater emphasis on team games and the development of fundamental skills used in games.

In order to serve the needs and interests of the children from the kindergarten through the sixth grade, the play areas should be close to the building and readily accessible to the elementary classroom. The elementary physical education and recreation and recreation area should have a minimum of 4 acres for 300 pupils and 1/2 additional acre for each additional 100 pupils.

The kindergarten children should have a section of the elementary-school play area of not less than 5,000 square feet set aside for their use. This area should be separated from the other areas by a fence or hedge and should include: (1) a grassy play area; (2) a small surfaced area; (3) a shaded area; and (4) an apparatus area.

The small area of asphalt or all-weather surface, not smaller than a classroom, should be adjacent to the doorway. In this outdoor area, the children can play when the other grassy areas are wet and muddy. It has been found very practical to locate a playhouse adjacent to this surfaced area, to store such equipment as large outdoor blocks, planks, and sawhorses.

The shaded area should be a part of every kindergarten area, for here is where the teacher can do her straitening. It is very desirable to place in this area such apparatus as climbing structures, horizontal bars, horizontal ladders, and rings. The landing space under all apparatus should be filled with a resilient material such as sand and tanbark, sawdust, or shavings.

Many schools provide separate primary and intermediate-grade play areas. This is very desirable and should be done whenever possible. Both of these play areas should include essentially the same four areas we have just described.

The turf area, for informal and free play and for relatively unorganized games, has to be large enough to include separate areas where the pupils of the fifth and sixth grades can play such games as softball, field ball, line soccer, and other lead-up games.

The asphalt area should be of sufficient size for the same activities that are performed in the gymnasium or playroom. Various markings can be painted on this surfacing, such as different-size circles, hopscotch, shuffleboard courts, and so on. If net games of the lead-up variety are desired, they should be similar to the secondary-school facilities that will be discussed later.

The apparatus area should be so located that it does not break up any large grassy area and, whenever possible, should be a shaded spot. It is desirable to have two separate playground apparatus areas each with the proper size equipment. When selecting apparatus, developmental equipment should be preferred to the recreational type.

Secondary Schools

The program for junior-high school girls should provide a broad foundation in physical education skills upon which can be based the more highly specialized instruction and practice included in the seniority school program, such as archery, golf, volleyball, tennis, field hockey, speakable, and softball.

The program for junior-high school boys should offer opportunities for instruction and practice in a variety of activities. An intramural program should supplement the instructional program. Some schools have limited competition in certain types of extramural athletics.

The physical education facilities should be as near the gymnasium and dressing rooms and showers as possible, yet far enough away from the classrooms to prevent playground noise interfering with classroom instruction. Pupils should not have to cross streets, roadways, or driveways when passing from the building to the play areas. The facilities should be accessible to parking areas for the convenience of the community, however.

Four distinct play areas are necessary for good physical education and recreation programs in junior and senior-high schools: (1) courts; (2) high-school girls area; (3) high-school boys area; and (4) inter-school athletic area.

The Courts Area.

The courts should be near the gymnasium and as near the parking facilities as possible. It is desirable to set the net posts in sleeves which are embedded in concrete, so that the posts may be removed and the sleeves capped. This permits the area to be used for many other games and for skating in the winter. Lines of various colors can be painted on the asphalt, a different color for each sport. It is important that the area be fenced. Walls should be erected at one end for handball and the volleying of tennis balls. The area will also provide space for such activities as volleyball and badminton. Many schools equip this area with lights so that the recreation program on summer nights can include sports and dancing. The area will also make excellent outdoor teaching stations when the other areas are wet and muddy.

High-School Girls Area.

It is necessary to have a separate area for high-school girls if they are going to have equal opportunities to participate in an adequate physical education program. This space should be located as near the building as possible so that a minimum amount of time is lost going to and from the dressing room and showering room.

The size of the area will depend on the enrollment, but there should be sufficient space for one full-sized official field for such organized games as field hockey, soccer, lacrosse, and softball. There also should be some additional space for the teaching of archery. This should be an isolated area. It is a very important safety precaution to teach archery where there are no pupils who are not participating. If a golf driving range is included in the facilities, the same precautions should be taken.

This area will be used by the girls for class-instruction, and for intramural and inter-school activities at other times.

High School Boys Area.

This area should be separate from the high-school girls area and the inter-school athletic area to avoid scheduling problems. It should be as close as possible to the dressing room and showering room. There should be sufficient space for such activities as softball, soccer, football, speakable, touch football, and lacrosse.

The same principles that apply to the planning of the high-school girls area hold here.

Inter-school Athletic Area.

Since this area sometimes holds the community's only athletic facilities, it should be planned for both school and community use. The type of interscholastic program that is offered will determine to a great extent the kind and number of playing areas. If the school is of sufficient size the following areas should be provided: a football field and several additional practice fields. These areas will also allow for jumping pits, pole-vaulting pits and so on.

Principles in Planning

If the outdoor facilities are going to be functional, then certain basic principles should be used when planning any outdoor areas. Some of these guiding principles are:

1. Never plan two activities that are played in the same sports season in the same area.

2. Locate such playing areas as soccer fields, football fields, and tennis courts as nearly as possible in a north-south direction, so that the sun will not shine directly in the participants eyes.

3. Locate the softball and baseball diamonds in one of the following positions so that the sun does not shine in the participants eyes: The terrain may determine which of the following settings to use:

The best setting would have the line passion from the pitcher's box to home base form an angle of 20^0 NE with the long axis that is due north and south.

The second best setting would have the line passing from the pitcher's box to home base form an angle of 20^0 SW with the long axis that is due north and south.

The third-best setting would have the line passing from the pitcher's box to home base form an angle of 45^0 SW with the long axis that is due north and south.

1. Locate the following areas in the indicated order of proximity to the school building, so that time may be saved throughout the school day:

Instructional area

Intramural area

Inter-school area

2. Locate the outdoor play areas so that pupils do not have to cross any driveways, roadways, or lanes of traffic in order to get to them.

3. Develop the courts area as a multiple-purposc area in order to save space and money.

4. Plan for three separate playground areas whenever possible in the elementary grades:

Kindergarten area

Primary area

Intermediate area

Facilities: Situations and Analysis

First Situation: Dressing Rooms and Showering Rooms

As a new director of physical education in Elmhurst Public Schools you are reviewing the proposed building plans for three new elementary schools. You notice that no dressing rooms and showers are proposed for any of the schools. Mr. Bennett, the superintendent of schools, has indicated that they are not being included because the dressing and showering facilities in a school built just two years ago are not being used.

Questions

At what grade level should dressing and showering be initiated? Why is it important to introduce dressing and showering to pupils in the elementary grades? What type of facilities are needed for carrying on an adequate program of dressing and showering in the elementary grades? Do these facilities have any value for outside groups who may use the school's facilities after school hours? Can you justify not building dressing rooms and showers in new schools because they are not being used in your older schools?

Analysis

It has been found by many elementary schools that a dressing and showering program can be very successfully initiated at the third or fourth-grade level. It is not a problem of getting pupils at these grade levels into the shower, but a problem of getting them out of the shower.

Since it is a desirable health practice to dress properly for physical activities and to shower after physical activity, it is the responsibility of the school to offer the facilities to their pupils. If these health practices are to be inculcates, they should be initiated early, when youngsters are ready. When dressing and showering are introduced in the elementary grades, there are fewer problems with the pupils when they reach the junior and senior-high-school grades, because they have already acquired these desirable health practices.

The only facilities needed are two dressing and showering facilities, one for boys and one for girls. In an elementary school of approximately 600 pupils this would mean four rooms about the same size as four classrooms. Two would be showering rooms equipped with a sufficient number of showed heads, and two would be dressing rooms equipped with an adequate number of lockers. In many communities the elementary schools are used as neighborhood recreation centers for adult recreational and educational programs. With dressing rooms and showers available, a more desirable adult program may be conducted.

It is not justifiable to say that dressing and showering facilities should not be included in a new building program because they are not being used where they already exist. Since it is a desirable health practice to dress and shower, and since the schools have the facilities, it is the responsibility of both the superintendent of schools and the director of physical education to see that this part of the program is implemented. You, as the new director of physical education, should investigate why this has not been done. Is the principal having trouble scheduling time for dressing and showering? Is there a lack of interest on the part of the physical education teachers? After making a thorough investigation, you should have another meeting with Mr. Bennett, to explain the necessity of having dressing rooms and showers in the new schools and of initiating their use where they already exist.

Second Situation: Limited Indoor Facilities

Mr. Whitney, the director of physical education, has been informed by the superintendent of schools that, until the new building program at the high school has been completed, the indoor physical education some suggestions as to what type of program can be scheduled during periods of inclement weather.

Question

What are considered limited indoor physical education facilities? With limited indoor facilities, what program could be conducted during inclement weather? Should the adjustments in physical education made during the building program be continued after adequate facilities become available?

Analysis

Indoor physical education facilities are considered limited when they can accommodate only a few activities and a minimum number of classes per week. Also limited are the number of activities in the intramural and interscholastic programs and the number of pupils who can participate in them.

During good weather the physical education classes may be held in the outdoor facilities. During inclement weather, use can be made of regular classrooms to teach the knowledge-and-appreciation aspects of physical education. Textbooks, films, and filmstrips may be used to supplement this phase of physical education. Since knowledge is one of the objectives of physical education, such instruction should be continued even after the building program has been completed.

Third Situation: Partitioning the Gymnasium

The new building program in Oakland last year included a gymnasium in the new high school, with a soundproof folding partition which would create two teaching stations. Because of the rise in the cost of construction it was impossible to put in the partition. It has been suggested that some substitute for the partition, such as a curtain or net be used.

Questions

When installing a folding partition in a gymnasium, what are some of the factors to be considered? Can a net or curtain serve as an adequate substitute for the partition?

Analysis

Folding partitions are installed in order to create separate teaching stations in a gymnasium. Therefore, they should be soundproof and extend from the floor to the ceiling. When they are retracted, they should be recessed in a well, so they do not become a hazard. There should be a door in the partition so that one can pass from one teaching station to the other without leaving the gymnasium.

Curtains and nets are poor substitutes for a soundproof folding partition. It would be very difficult to teach different activities in a large gymnasium divided only by curtains or nets, because of the noise. Oakland High School should save its money and not purchase curtains or nets. When monies are available, they should purchase the folding partition.

Forth Situation: Planning The Courts Area

Mr. Gaffney, the superintendent of schools in Maplewood, has told Mr. Gaines, the director of physical education, that can plan for 10 tennis courts at the new senior-high school for 1,000 pupils. There is plenty of usable space for these courts, so there is no problem about their location, but Mr. Gaines is wondering whether it would be better to have 10 courts side or two rows of 5 courts placed back to back.

Question

Are 10 tennis courts adequate? Where should they be locate? What direction should they face? Is it more economical to place tennis courts side by side or back or back to back?

Analysis

Ten tennis courts can accommodate a maximum of 40 pupils participating in a regular game of tennis. For instructional periods and practice of skills, it would be possible to have more pupils participating. For class instruction, 10 courts would be sufficient for a school of 1,000 pupils. Whether they are sufficient for the extra-class program will depend on how extensive the intramural and Inter-school programs are. Since there is plenty of usable land, there would be no problem about finding space for additional courts at a later date if they were needed.

For supervisory purposes the tennis courts should be located near other playing areas, but still far enough away so that the pupils will not be hit by each other's balls, bats, and other supplies. This means they will be near the school and close to the parking facilities. The tennis courts should be placed in a north-south direction so that the participants are not facing into the sun.

Considerable money could be saved by placing the courts side by side because they would need less surfacing and fencing. Since there is plenty of space, Mr. Gaines should recommend to Mr. Gaffney that the courts be placed side by side.

Fifth Situation: Gymnasium Courts

After the new high-school gymnasium at Harrisville was constructed, the superintendent of schools asked the director of physical education to draw up plans for marking the floor. The director discovered that the gymnasium was not quite the right size or shape and that he consequently must choose between a limited number of regulation courts or a sufficient number of less-than regulation court size.

Question

Should plans for marking the gymnasium floor be made prior to the construction of the gymnasium? What is the actual size and shape of the gymnasium? What adjustments can be made?

Analysis

All plans for gymnasiums should be based on the program to be conducted in this facility; therefore, all floor markings should have been planned well in advance of the actual construction of the gymnasium.

The actual usable floor space is 100 by 100 feet. It should be noted that every indoors playing area for high-school pupils is rectangular including courts for basketball, volleyball, badminton, and shuffleboard. It is impossible to put these regulation rectangular courts into a square gymnasium 100 by 100 feet and utilize all the space. It would be better to have a rectangular gymnasium, 84 by 104 feet.

It is possible to reduce the larger courts, such as the basketball and volleyball courts, by a few feet without affecting the actual game. However, a smaller court, such as a badminton court, should not be reduced more than 2 feet in length or 1 foot in width. The minimum recommended safety lanes between courts and between courts and walls should not be reduced. Teachers who do not want many different colored lines on the floor could put down tape for the courts as they need them. This can be made simple by painting on the floor the right angles at the end lines for each of the courts.

6

PUBLIC RELATIONS

There is general agreement among authors that today's concept of public relations grew out of the word publicity. In order to gain public understanding and support from the community, however, it is necessary to do more than publicize the program of physical education.

It is necessary to make use of the many desirable methods of leading public opinion toward intelligent group action and support of the physical education program. This makes it necessary to create a two-way avenue for communication, so that information and understanding can travel between the personnel in the schools and the citizens of the community.

The Functions of Public Relations

Some of the more important functions of public relations, as they relate to the physical education program, are;

1. To keep the community properly informed about all parts of the physical education program.

2. To develop an awareness of the need for a good physical education program in the total education curriculum.

3. To gain support for adequate facilities, sufficient teaching time, and qualified personnel.

4. To promote the concept of the united action of teachers and parents for a better physical education program.

5. To evaluate the physical education program as to whether it is meeting the needs of pupils in the community.

6. To avoid any misunderstandings about the aims and objectives of the physical education program.

Principles of Public Relations

A good public relations program for physical education must be based on sound principles:

1. Accuracy.

2. Awareness of the fact that there are many different publics, with varying interests and problems.

3. A good physical education program.

4. Continuity.

5. Two-way communication of information between the school and the community.

6. A knowledge of what the community thinks about the physical education program.

7. Involvement of all school personnel.

Communication With Various Publics

Physical education is often questioned as an academic subject, and so is its place in the total educational program. Although everyone outside of the field claims to know something about it, the interesting fact is that people know very little about physical education. Many misconceptions and half-truths handicap the program of physical education. There are several publics that need to know the facts. The best way to get the facts to them is for physical educators to communicate what is being done and what they hope to do. There are many ways that a physical educator can promote his program with the various publics. Some of these are:

1. Teach your pupils what physical education is and how it can help them. Proper communication with pupils will teach them what it means to be physically educated, and they will learn to appreciate and respect skilled movements and a strong, healthy body.

2. Keep the parents informed about what you are doing with their children in the physical education program. The average parent is as concerned with the class-instruction activities as he is with the extracts activities.

3. Socialize with other faculty members outside of physical education. Go to lunch with them, serve on committees, and make it a point to attend all faculty meetings. Try to learn what is happening in other educator should be sympathetic and understanding of others problems if he is to expect the same treatment from them.

4. Keep all administrators informed about the program of physical education. One of the best ways is for the physical education staff to develop a local course of study which is submitted to the administration and

board of education.

5. Inform the board of education about the physical education program, objectives, and problems. This can be done by presenting an annual report to the board of education and also by submitting copies of local course of study.

Public-Relations Media

There are numerous media of communications which can be used in a public-relations program. Two factors should determine what media should be used in a particular situation: (1) certain media have more significance than others in a particular community: and (2) certain media are more readily available than others. The physical education staff should make a survey of its situation to determine which media can be used and which will do the most effective job. However, it should never be forgotten that the best way of building good public relations is still through the program and the leadership.

Newspapers

The newspaper is one most common and useful media for disseminating information. It reaches many people and can be of great assistance in interpreting the physical education program to the community. When preparing news stories:

1. State only the facts.

2. Tell the story briefly.

3. Make the report coherent and accurate.

4. Punctuate and paragraph correctly.

5. Avoid abbreviations, slang, wordiness, and involved sentences.

6. Type the copy with double spacing.

7. Make sure that your story is in on time.

Films

Films are a very effective way of presenting a story in a short period of time. The 8 and 16 millimeter film can be used by the physical education staff to show the public exactly what is being done in the physical education program. Movies can be taken of activities during physical education classes for showing at PTA meetings. Films are also a good instructional aid in working with pupils.

Photographs And Graphics

Both pictures and graphic illustrations are very effective. Photographs should show action and include people: Action pictures are more appealing than static ones and pictures with people in them are more effective than pictures that do not have people. Usually, a few people are better than many persons. E.g., physical fitness scores and number of participants in the intramural and interscholastic activities–can be made more interesting and appealing if they are presented in graphs, charts, and profiles.

Public Speeches

Making speeches to the public can be a very effective medium for public relations. A good speech will often do much to inform the public about the physical education program. To develop an effective speech:

1. Know the purpose of the speech.

2. Know what public will be listening.

3. Prepare a general outline of the speech.

4. Research and collect information for the speech.

5. Prepare a more detailed outline of the speech.

6. Practice the speech.

Live Demonstrations

Demonstrations at which all pupils perform are an entertaining and informative medium for public relations. For an effective presentation:

1. Use student leaders for demonstration purposes, to demonstrate your teaching of leadership.

2. Make the demonstration dynamic, interesting, and informative.

3. Explain the objectives of the program as the pupils perform.

4. Make sure that all safety precautions have been followed.

5. Keep the program short enough so that it doesn't drag.

Radio and Television

Because of their universal appeal, radio and television are very effective means of communication. These media offer the best opportunity to reach the greatest number of people at one time. Some radio and television stations will make free time available as a public service. In some communities there are educational radio and television stations. Some schools are fortunate enough to have stations of their own.

Displays

Posters, exhibits, and brochures can be used to advertise, promote, announce, recognize, and dramatize the program. Almost every school has bulletin boards in the physical education areas. Very effective use can be made of these bulletin boards by;

1. Making the display attractive, bright, colorful, and eye-catching.

2. Using clippings and pictures.

3. Printing in large letters.

4. Posting up-to-date information about activities, times, places, persons to see.

Public Relations: Situations and Analysis

First Situation: A Football Film

Mr. Gainey, the superintendent of schools, has asked Mr. Sager, the director of physical education, to show the film of last Saturday's football game to the Rotary, Club on Thursday evening. He has indicated to Mr. Sager that this would be an excellent means for explaining the physical education program to the public.

Questions

Is the showing of a film a desirable means of public relations? Why is it desirable to use public-relations media with community service organizations? Is the showing of a high-school football film the most desirable way of interpreting the physical education program to the public?

Analysis

Since a great many people enjoy watching films, it is one of the better ways of keeping the public well informed. Films are not only entertaining but also are an effective vehicle for information and education. Films can build up interest, capture attention, and stimulate thinking in ways not possible with printed materials. It is desirable to use public-relations media with community-service organizations because the members of such clubs are interested in the welfare of their children and in the schools.

Since many of these organizations ask school personnel to present programs at their meetings, they provide ready-made situations where publicity can be truly effective.

Generally speaking, members of service clubs are the leaders and influential people in the community. Because of their position and interest, they can do much to further a school's relation with the general public.

A high-school football film is one way to show part of the physical education program but showing only one activity is not the best way to interpret the physical education program to the public. A better procedure would be to show a film of boys and girl in all grades participating in many different activities in their everted physical education classes. Such a film would show class activities, intramural, and interscholastics.

Second Situation: Star Performers

Mr. Doherty, the principal of the Henry C. Calhoun Elementary School, wants the parents to have a better understanding of the various special educational programs in his school. He is asking Miss Carr, the physical education teacher, to have a few highly skilled pupils perform for the P.T.A. Miss Carr questions whether this approach will promote the best public relations.

Questions

Is the use of a few skilled performers the best way of informing the public about the program of physical education? What other ways can pupils be used to inform the public about physical education?

Analysis

The use of a few skilled performers is one way of communicating the physical education program to the public. The limitation of this method, well exemplified by interscholastic athletics, is that you reach a limited number of parents and are usually presenting only a limited portion of the program. When only a few skilled performers and a limited number of activities are presented, the public is misinformed about the total physical education program.

There are several other ways that pupils may be used to inform the public about physical education. Probably the best advertisement for the school is the child who goes home each day happy, motivated, and well-informed. This can only be accomplished with a curriculum that meets his interests and needs, and challenges his capacities—and a well-taught, broad physical education program including many activities is an essential part of such a curriculum.

Live demonstrations at P.T.A. Meetings, open house, and other school community functions are an excellent means of using the pupils to communicate with the public.

These demonstrations should include all pupils in the everyday classes, however, and not just the highly skilled. The intramural program is a valuable part of the extra-class program and it can also be used effectively to better inform the public. A few of the intramural contests for boys and girls should be scheduled in the evening, so parents can attend.

Third Situation: Bulletin Boards

Mr. Beam, the director of physical education, is concerned because the physical education teachers in his two senior-high schools and sixty-nine-high schools are not using the physical education bulletin boards as a means of promoting the program of physical education.

Questions

What use can be made of the bulletin boards as a means of public relations? What factors should be considered?

Analysis

Since bulletin boards are generally strategically located near the gymnasium or the dressing and showering facilities, they can be very effectively used for public relations. Among the many uses of a bulletin board are: advertising, promotions, announcements, recognition, and dramatization. Probably the best use of bulletin boards however, is to display educational materials. Such information as the position of players, the location of facilities, supplies, and equipment, and the meaning of terminology can be presented.

Unfortunately, too few bulletin boards display such materials.

Certain factors make for an effective bulletin board. Materials should be attractive, bright, colorful, and eye-catching. The printing or writing should be in large enough letters to be readable at short distances.

The bulletin board should be kept up-to-date by changing the information about different schedules, places, persons, and activities each season.

Fourth Situation: Showers

Miss Welker, the physical education teacher at Cooperstown High School, would like to have all girls shower at the end of the physical education classes now that adequate facilities are available in the new high school. After the first week of classes, Miss Welker has noticed that many girls are not taking showers.

Questions

What are the first steps that Miss Welker should take in order to properly implement the showering phase of the program? What action should she take with the pupils who are not showering? Besides the pupils, what other people should be informed about showering as an integral part of the program?

Analysis

In order to properly implement the showering phase of the program, Miss Welker should first discuss the value of this program with the pupils. She should check to see if facilities exist in the elementary grades and junior-high school grades, and whether the girls are using them.

Miss Welker should find out why the girls are not taking showers. It may be that then feel too rushed. The teacher should then allocate more time if she feels that this is a reasonable complaint.

If it is a question of modesty, individual stall showers would help. If they are not available and not many girls are affected, these girls might be excused early so that they could shower before the rest of the class.

Parents should be informed that showering is an integral part of the program, because many times the problem is not with the child but with the parents.

It is easier to carry out any program if the teacher has the cooperation of both the parent and the child.

Fifth Situation: A P.T.A. Talk

Mrs. Bigsbee, the physical education teacher in Fly Creek Elementary School, has been asked by her principal, Mr. Herman, to give a speech at the next P.T.A. Meeting on the value of a good physical education program.

Questions

What can Mrs. Bigsbee do to help develop an effective speech? What are some of the fundamentals of a good speech?

Analysis

There are several things Mrs. Bigsbee can do to help develop an effective speech. First, she must decide the purpose of her speech and find out who will be her audience. Then she should prepare a general outline of her speech. Once this is done, she should read the literature and start to glean information for the speech. She could then develop a more detailed outline of her speech. Lest, she should practice the speech several times.

There are several fundamentals of a good speech. The speaker should know his subject thoroughly. He should exhibit great interest in and enthusiasm for his topic. His main effort should be to put ideas and facts across to the audience, rather than to put himself across. The speech should be well prepares, direct, not too lengthy, and clear.

Sixth Situation: A Newspaper Story

Mr. Ravena, the new director of physical education in the Batavia City School district, has noticed that there are several errors in an article about the physical education program in the city newspaper.

Questions

What steps should be taken by the director of physical education to insure that a newspaper story is accurate? What sources of information should reporters use in writing articles about physical education?

Analysis

Because the newspaper is one of the most common and useful media for informing the public, great care should be taken to insure accuracy. The director of physical education should keep the story brief and state only the facts. After it has been written it should be checked to see that it is coherent, properly punctuated, and paragraphed correctly. Abbreviations, slang, wordiness, and involved sentences should be avoided.

The final copy should be typewritten, with double spacing, and submitted on time. There are various sources of information available to reporters who may write articles about physical education.

Physical education teachers can be encouraged to write about the physical education activities in their schools. The coaches of interscholastic athletics can give first-hand information about their teams. All stories should clear through the school principal, the director of physical education, and the superintendent before release.

7

EVALUATION

Evaluation is becoming more recognized as a necessary and integral part of the physical education program. There is an increasing awareness that in order to demonstrate the benefits of a physical education program and in order to conduct it in the most efficient way, measurement and evaluation are necessary. Measurement and evaluation are highly related, but they are not equivalent.

Evaluation is border than measurement. Measurement merely indicates status by answering such questions as how much, how often, and how many; evaluation on the other hand, goes beyond the pure mechanics of testing and measuring. It is an appraisal of the results of measurement in terms of aims and objectives, and it is important that evaluation include a follow-up .

As a consequence of evaluation, objectives may be changed, programs revised, facilities improved, staff increased and methodology changed–all to create a better teaching and learning situation for the pupil. In order for evaluation to be successful, however, it must be continuous.

Both the product and the process have to be

measured frequently. There are still some physical educators who doubt that educational outcomes can be evaluated.

This misconception has existed among educators for many years. It was about a half-century ago that, because of this attitude, Edward Lee Thorndike made his famous statement that whatever exists at all exists in amounts and that anything that exists in amounts can be measured. Not all measurement in physical education is objective.

Much of it is not as simple as the tests which give results in terms of inches, feet, seconds, and minutes. There are some characteristics which are impossible to measure objectively; consequently, results cannot be expressed in quantitative terms and the measurement is subjective and frequently less reliable than objectively determined results.

The challenge to physical educators is to make such measurements as objective and systematic as possible, so that they will have greater reliability. Qualities and factors that are not readily isolated or identified are difficult to measure and can only be expresses in qualitative terms.

The Purposes of Measurement and Evaluation

The function of measurement in the school today must keep pace with our changing philosophy of education. Modern education demands that each child be given the opportunity to progress as rapidly as he can or as slowly as he must. Physical education is a continuous process in which, with skillful teaching, the development of the child is guided on the basis of the speed, direction, and extent of his previous growth. If the maximum growth and development of each child is to be the main goal of our physical education program, then frequent measures of each child's physical fitness, skills, knowledge, and social competence must be made.

The primary purpose of measurement and evaluation is to assess status, and thus identify progress or achievement. Some of the secondary uses of measurement devices and evaluation techniques are:

1. To classify pupils.
2. To use in counseling pupils.
3. To motivate pupils.
4. To contribute to research.
5. To use for marking purposes.

Types of Measuring Instruments

There are several devices available for the evaluation of physical education. All are useful, but some are popular than others:

Observation. Observation is a very good technique if the teacher knows what to look for. Such instruments as score cards and rating scales can make observations more objective.

Check Lists. A simple list of important items to look for when engaged in appraising pupils makes for more objective and worthwhile evaluation.

Interviews. An effective measuring device which can be quite effective in determining how pupils feel about various parts of the physical education program.

Records. Cumulative records are a necessity if the teacher is to determine the pupil's status and progress.

Tests. These are the most common means of appraising the pupil's status and progress. They should include tests of physical fitness, knowledge, and skills.

The Selection of Appropriate Tests

Standardized tests should not be administered merely because testing is the current educational fad. Nor should a test be administered simple because it is a good test; It should be good for a specific purpose. Appropriate tests must be chosen if best use is to be made of the results. The choices should be made in the light of the objectives sought.

Competencies Needed in Evaluation

Evaluations must be made by qualified personnel if they are to be effective. There are certain competencies that both beginning and experienced teachers must have in order to conduct a desirable program of measurement. Barrow and McGee have indicated that a physical education teacher must be competent in the following area:

Knowledge of Where to Locate Tests. First, the teacher must know what measurement instruments are available and where the information for their effective use may be found.

Knowledge of How to Evaluate Tests. Second, the teacher must know how to properly evaluate the tests which are being used.

Knowledge of How to Administer Tests. Third, when the appropriate instrument has been selected, the teacher must be able to administer the measurement program so that the resulting data will be valid and reliable and so that there is no waste of valuable time.

Knowledge of How to Interpret Test Results. Fourth, the teacher must be able to interpret what test scores mean when they are obtained.

Knowledge of How to Use Test Results. Fifth, the teacher must have knowledge of the use that can be made of measurement results so that the effectiveness of the program can be improved.

Knowledge of How to Construct Written and Motor Performance Tests. Sixth, the teacher should be able to construct scientifically teacher-made tests.

Knowledge of How to Use Elementary Statistics. Seventh, in order to interpret test results, to develop norms, and to construct homemade tests, the teacher must know how to use elementary statistics.

Knowledge of How Evaluation Relates to the Total Program. Eighth, the teacher must be able to see the relationship between evaluation and the physical education program.

Evaluation: Situations and Analysis

First Situation: Evaluating Many Pupils

Mr. Jenkins is the only physical education teacher in the two elementary schools in Brownsville. He teaches all pupils in grades 1 to 6 in each school, which means he teaches approximately 1,200 different pupils every week. He has been asked by the elementary-school principal to make an evaluation of each pupil's progress in physical education.

Questions

How is a pupil's status and progress in physical education determined? Can a person who teaches 1,200 different pupils every week evaluate them acquittal? Are there measuring instruments adequate for determining a pupil's status and progress in physical education at the elementary-grade level? Should the elementary-classroom teacher also be involved in evaluating the pupils physical education?

Analysis

The evaluation of a pupil's status and progress in physical education should be based upon the recognized objectives of physical education, such as physical fitness, skills, knowledge, and social competence. It would not be possible for Mr. Jenkins to make an adequate evaluation of 1,200 pupils.

In fact, it would be almost impossible for a teacher even to know the names of 1,200 different pupils when he teaches them only once a week. Some standardized tests are available for measuring the physical fitness of intermediate-grade pupils.

Like other teachers, the physical educator must use teacher-made tests to measure skills and knowledge.

In addition he must subjectively evaluate the social competence of pupils, just as the elementary-classroom teacher does. The physical educator's evaluation of the status and progress of primary-grade pupils must be subjective. Anecdotal reports may be made to parents. It is generally agreed that the elementary-classroom teacher should supplement the teaching of physical education by the physical educator.

Since the elementary-classroom teacher should be teaching some of the physical education to her pupils, she should be involved in evaluating her pupil's status and progress in physical education. The cooperative effort of both the physical educator and the classroom teacher will result in a sound and comprehensive evaluation of the pupils.

Second Situation: A Marking Plan

The physical education teachers at Hudson High School have been asked to submit a plan to the high-school principal for marking pupils in physical education. Mr. Raush, the directory of physical education, has asked his staff to come to its monthly meeting next Tuesday with some suggestions.

Questions

What factors should be considered by the staff in developing a marking system for physical education? Should a marking system be numerical, letter, or Satisfactory–Unsatisfactory? Should the physical education mark be included in figuring averages for the honor roll?

Analysis

The marking system should be based upon the objectives of physical education and should include the following: physical fitness, skills, knowledge, and social competence. These aspects of performance may be measured subjectively as well as objectively. The staff must determine what weight to give each of these objectives in determining a mark in physical education, by deciding their relative value. A marking system for physical education in a school should be consistent with the marking system in other subjects. If English, social studies, and science are marked numerically, then physical education should be marked numerically.

Since physical education is part of the total curriculum and can be measured like other subjects, it should be included with other subjects in figuring the average for the honor roll. Pupils must be totally educated, in both mind and body, and it is imperative to avoid dichotomizing the individual.

Third Situation: Criteria For Marks

Mr. Lyons, the director of health and physical education, has been told by the superintendent of schools that board of education is willing to grant credit for high-school physical education if the staff can show them a sound working system. At present, the only test administered to the classes is the AAHPERD Fitness Test.

Questions

What objectives of physical education should the marking system be based upon? What weight should be given to each objective in figuring the final mark? Are there standardized tests to measure a pupil's status and progress in physical education? Should a mark be given in physical education even though credit is not granted?

Analysis

Physical education marks should be based upon the

recognized objectives of physical education, including physical fitness, skills, knowledge, and social competence. The weight given each objective should reflect the philosophy of the physical education staff.

Therefore, Mr. Lyons should discuss with his staff what objectives should be considered and what weight should be given to each one. There are some standardized tests for the measurement of the physical fitness, skills, and knowledge of high-school students.

There are also ways of measuring social competence, including sociometric techniques. In order to have a sound marking system, the tests administered should be appropriate for all objectives, not just physical fitness.

Marks are given in other subjects. In order for physical education to be recognized as part of the total educational curriculum, marks should be given in physical education whether credit is granted or not.

Fourth Situation: Reporting test Scores to Parents

The physical education staff at Harper High School administers the AAHPERD Fitness Test to all pupils. The administration has asked the staff how the findings can best be interpreted to the parents and who should communicate the information.

Questions

What means of communication does the school have with parents? Can physical fitness test results best be communicated orally, in writing, or both? Who should have the responsibility for interpreting physical-fitness test results to the parents?

There are severe means of communication that school personnel have with parents, including conferences, P.T.A. Meetings, report cards, demonstrations, progress reports, and television and radio programs. One of the most effective ways of interpreting any phase of physical education is by demonstration. Probably, both oral and written communication of test results should be used.

An excellent technique for informing parents of their pupil's progress in physical fitness is to send home a report explaining the test and the results of their child's performance. Both the administration and the physical education staff have the responsibility for communicating with the parents about all phases of the physical education program.

However, because of the technical nature of the interpretation of physical fitness test scores, this responsibility should belong to the physical education staff, which has the requisite professional background.

Fifth Situation: Physical-Fitness Tests

At a physical education staff meeting there is a discussion of physical-fitness testing. One of the teachers says that a real good test of physical fitness is the Rogers Physical Fitness Index and that it should be administered throughout the school district for both boys and girls. Another teacher disagrees and states that a better test for measuring the physical fitness of boys and girls is Larson's Dynamic Strength Test. The final decision must be made by Mr. Phelan, the director of physical education. What test should he select?

Questions

For what grade level are these tests recommended? Are they recon mended for both boys and girls? Do they require expensive equipment? Can they be administered in minimum amount of time? What components of physical fitness do they measure?

Analysis

The Rogers Physical fitness Index is recommended for boys and girls, ages 8 to 18. The Larson dynamic Strength Test is recommended for high school boys only. On this basis, the better test for Mr. Phelan would be the Rogers Physical Fitness Index.

With it, his school district could measure the performance of all pupils in grades 4 to 12 with the same test. The Rogers physical Fitness Index takes a considerable amount of expensive equipment, however, and it takes a great deal of time to administer and score, while the Larson Dynamic Strength Test uses only the high horizontal bar and the parallel bars, which most high schools should have. This test is much shorter than the Physical Fitness Index and therefore can be given in much less time. Both tests chiefly measure strength, and the newer concept of physical fitness is broader.

Other factors, such as agility, speed, and endurance, should be considered components of physical fitness. Mr. Phelan should therefore look for a more comprehensive test than either of the two suggested at the meeting.

Sixth Situation: Failing in Physical Education

Sally Smith, a senior in Jonesville High School, has

received a failing mark in physical education. Her parents are quite concerned because it is the only course she is failing and it is keeping her off the honor roll.

They have contacted Mr. Kinsey, the high school principal, who invited them to the school to talk to Miss Burns, the physical education teacher.

Questions

What should constitute a passing mark in physical education? Has the school informed the parents as to what is passing or failing in physical education? Had Sally's parents been informed previous to this marking period as to her status in physical education?

Analysis

Marks in physical education should be based upon the objectives of the program. Therefore, tests and other evaluative techniques should be used to measure physical fitness, skills, knowledge, and social competence.

All of these evaluative techniques should take into consideration individual differences among pupils. A pupil who attends class, participates in the activities, cooperates, and works to his capacity should be able to attain the minimum standard for passing physical education. The school should inform the parents about the physical education program including policies pursuant to such topics as passing and failing.

This can be done in a number of different ways, including parent conferences, letters, and handbooks. Another source of information that would assist parents as well as other teachers, board of education members, and administrators in the understanding of physical education is a local course of study.

There should be a periodic report of pupil status and progress sent to the parents so that they are informed. Prior to receiving a failing grade in physical education, there should have been conferences between the pupil and Miss Burns and also between Sally's parents and Miss Burns.

8

ELEMENTARY AND SECONDARY-SCHOOL CLASS AND EXTRA CLASS PROGRAMS

The Physical Education Class Program

The program of physical education should be based on the needs of individual pupils and the communities where they live, and planned and conducted so that it contributes to the fulfillment of the purposes of education and the objectives of physical education.

The Philosophy of Physical Education

One of the major needs of man has always been the need for movement. Physical activity is a constructive force, essential to the growth and development of all children and youth. Such elements as heredity, rest, sleep, diet, and many others effect the functioning of the whole person and, as such, are known as conditioning factors. These contributing factors form the basis upon which, through physical activity, such qualities as coordination, strength, balance, speed, and endurance can be developed.

In order to insure youth an opportunity to be physically fit, it is necessary to make adequate provision for physical activities in their everyday living. The biological urge for physical activity is nature's way of developing children and youth. The basic design for mankind has not changed: He is still meant to be the active, spirited organism that he has always been, However, the changes in civilization in the past few decades, and the coming of the age of automation, have made man less physically active than ever before in his history. Without vigorous activities our children will develop neither physically nor mentally as they should.

The human being cannot be divided into a mind and a body. All our physical, emotional, and social qualities are so interrelated that they are impossible to separate. Physical education, as a part of the total educational program, has as its purpose to develop the whole child so that he is able to become a physically, mentally, emotionally, and socially fit citizen.

Program Planning

The program should be diversified so that it can offer the best possible opportunities for the growth and development of the pupils. This requires that there be many activities and that they be introduced at the appropriate grade and growth level.

For the sake of convenience, physical education class-instruction activities are grouped into the following categories:

1. Gemers. Includes team, individual, and dual.

2. Self-testing. Includes stunts, tumbling, and apparatus.

3. Dance. Includes basic rhythms, folk, square, modern, and social.

4. Body mechanics. Includes standing, walking, and running.

5. Aquatics. Includes swimming, diving, and water safety.

Remedial and adaptive.

Each school district should have a written course of study that will help give direction to program and provide for progression and continuity in class instruction throughout all grades. This guide should reflect the philosophy of the school administration and the physical education staff and their view of the place of physical education in the total curriculum.

The planning and development of the guide should be primarily the work of the teachers and administrators. After it has been approved by the administration and board of education, the teachers should use it as a guide in the conduct of the program. Each type of activity makes a certain contribution to the objectives of physical education.

It is therefore necessary to offer all these types of activities. Each pupil should receive instruction not only in skills that he can use during his school years but in other skills, as well, that may be used during his lifetime. The following general recommendations may be used as guidelines in planning the physical education program:

1. Adequate time, staff, and facilities should be available for the program planned.

2. Pupils and teachers should dress in a costume that is appropriate to the activities being taught and

which permits safe participation in the activities.

3. Showering, an integral part of the health and physical education program, should be required of all pupils who have participated in vigorous physical activity.

4. The program should provide for instruction in the proper care of equipment, supplies, lockers, and contents, and in the proper use of toilet, dressing, and showering facilities.

5. Such activities as dance lessons, band, R.O.T.C. and drill teams should not be accepted as substitutes for physical education.

6. Elementary-grade pupils should not be denied opportunities for participating in the physical education program because they have misbehaved in the classroom.

7. Pupils who are well enough to attend school should be considered well enough to attend physical education classes, but the teacher should adapt the activities to meet the individual pupil's needs, ranging from rest to limited participation.

8. The program should be based on the interests and needs of every boy and girl.

9. All pupils should participate in one or more parts of the physical education program daily.

10. Boys and girls should have equal opportunities to participate in a variety of activities.

11. Provision should be made for certain coeducational activities.

The Objectives of Physical Education

Physical activities, carefully selected and conducted under desirable leadership, contribute to the development of the physical fitness and motor skills of each pupil, as well as of his knowledge and appreciation an d social and democratic competence.

Knowledge and Appreciation of Physical Activities

Imparting a knowledge of physical activities and an appreciation of them should be an important aspect of the physical education program. All physical activities are learned; consequently, they involve thinking and result in the acquisition of knowledge. Besides the motor skills, every pupil should acquire a knowledge and appreciation of such things as rules, regulations, techniques, strategies, and the history of various physical activities. It is often easier to motivate pupils to seek knowledge through physical activities than through regular classroom assignments.

You can teach number concepts in the third grade, for example, using the game of "Steal the Bacon", and you can teach something about Holland by having the pupils in the fifth grade participate in a Dutch dance. The acquisition of knowledge about health is also an important part of the physical education program. Every pupil should know about such things as the importance of sanitation, factors in disease prevention, the importance of exercise, and the need for a well-balanced diet. This knowledge will contribute greatly to his general health and help him to live a more purposeful life.

The power to think quickly, to interpret a situation correctly, to make an accurate judgment, and to act on it may be developed on the playground and in the gymnasium. Participation in physical education activities will help each pupil to make the discriminatory decisions by which a knowledge of values is derived.

Physical Fitness

Physical education's unique contribution to the total curriculum is the building of physical power in each pupil through the development of the body. Physical fitness is the ability of the individual to sustain adaptive effort, the ability to recover, and the ability to resist fatigue.

Each pupil becomes more active, performs better, and is healthier if his body is adequately developed and functioning properly. The physical education program must provide for the physical development of all children.

No other area of the curriculum can meet this need. It is only through such natural activities as hanging, climbing, running, throwing, leaping, and jumping that adequate physical development is obtained.

The end result of these activities is that each individual has the vitality, strength, and endurance for routine work or play.

More he is prepared for the requirements and emergencies of everyday living, which may vary from year to year, month to month, week to week, or day to day.

Social Competence

Social competence involves the pupil's everyday

adjustments to other individuals and to his group. It is of the utmost importance that every child become socially competent, able to take his place and play his part as a worthy member of the community. Activities in the physical education program are an excellent medium for the development of an understanding and appreciation of human nature.

It is here that one of the best opportunities for making personal and group adjustment exists, if there is proper leadership. A pupil can learn to be a good sport only through experience, and no program offers more opportunities than physical education.

Motor Skills

Motor skills refer to the pupil's ability to perform physical movements with a minimum amount of energy and in a proficient and graceful manner. The program of physical education tries to develop in occupiable a variety of physical skills that he enjoys using and will enjoy in later life. It takes several years for most people to acquire coordination, and the most important period for its development is during the formative years.

Therefore, in order to attain skill it is necessary to start teaching many activities early in life and continue the teaching into adulthood. Skills not acquired during youth are often never acquired.

The physical education program should include the teaching of many skills when a person is young, and the teaching should progress throughout the school years.

The acquisition of motor skills is important for the citizen of tomorrow. As a people we are constantly experiencing an increase in our leisure time. What we do with this leisure will determine to a great extent the quality of our civilization.

One of the major tasks of the schools is to prepare youth to use their leisure well. The physical education program, by developing physical skills which may be enjoyed today and in the future, can make a major contribution.

Program Activities

All pupils should have opportunities for instruction and practice in physical education activities through class instruction in regularly scheduled physical education classes, special-activity classes when necessary, and extra-class activities.

The Extra-Class Program

Extra Class activities are those which are conducted outside the regularly scheduled class-instruction periods. The purpose of such activities is to enrich the class instruction with additional instruction, practice, and competition.

The administration and supervision of the extra-class program should be the responsibility of a physical educator, officially appointed and certified to teach or direct physical education.

Intramurals. Intramurals are those activities which are organized and conducted within one school and which include only those pupils enrolled in that school.

The word "intramural" is derived from the Latin intra, meaning "within, "and murals, meaning pertaining to a wall. These activities a natural outgrowth of the class instruction, should be voluntary. They are basically for pupils of moderate ability who are not participating in interscholastic competition.

Extramurals. Extramurals are those activities -sports days, play days, or other approved Inter-school activities- which are conducted without a season-long schedule, league competition, or championship.

On sports days, pupils from two or more schools participate in one or more activities but retain their school identity. On play days, pupils from two or more schools participate in one or more activities without retaining their school identity. This phase of the physical education program should also be voluntary. It is for pupils who want to play with and against pupils from other schools but who do not wish to play on a regularly scheduled interscholastic basis.

Interscholastics. Interscholastics are athletic activities which offer enriched opportunities for the more highly skilled pupils to represent a school in competition with pupils from other schools. These activities involve season-long schedules, organized practice, league competition, and championships, and are for pupils with above-average or exceptional athletic ability. This part of the physical education program is in line with the modern philosophy, which emphasizes the needs of the exceptional and talented student. Interscholastics require special facilities, special equipment, and special teachers to coach and supervise.

Extra-class Activities

For an extra-class program to be considered a good one, it must offer certain opportunities to pupils in all three phases of the extra-class program: intramurals; extramurals; and interscholastics.

Intramural activities. A good program of intramural activities will:

1. Offer coeducational opportunities in such activities as archery, badminton, bowling, golf, skiing, swimming, table tennis, and volleyball.

2. Organize leagues and tournaments in such a manner that there will be equal competition.

Frequently, schools will have a teacher select a captain for each team, and he, in turn, will select the players for his team. This is a good method of equating teams because pupils generally know the proficiency of their peers.

3. Provide adequate time for the use of facilities, preferably after school or on Saturdays. When after-school schedules conflict, it will be necessary to schedule intramurals during the noon hour or activity period.

4. Give all pupil an opportunity to choose from a variety of activities.

5. Encourage the participation of all pupils, including those who do not perform well.

6. Stress that the pleasure of participation is the main objective. There should be no excessive pressure to win.

7. Allow the pupils to participate in the planning and organizing of the intramural activities.

8. Exclude pupils who participate in the same sport on an interscholastic team.

9. Give careful consideration to scheduling the various activities so that pupils will receive prior instr ıction in the activity in the regular physical education classes. However when this instruction is not possible – e.g., for skiing and horseback riding the instruction should be come an integral part of the intramural program. Although the main purpose of the intramural activities is to promote the pupils participation, the teacher should be constantly alert to opportunities to teach additional skills and knowledge during the intramurals.

Extramural activities. A good program of extramural activities will:

1. Never be used as a substitute or replacement for intramural activities.

2. Exclude pupils who participate in the same sport on an interscholastic team.

3. Offer coeducational opportunities in such activities as archery, badminton, bowling golf, skiing, swimming, table tennis, tennis, and volleyball.

4. Offer a wide variety of activities to enrich the experiences of as many pupils as possible.

5. Stimulate many pupils to participate in the intramural activities.

6. Teach students to officiate and use them as officials during the games.

7. Include the transportation and the use of facilities in the regular scheduling of extra-class activities for boys and girls.

Interscholastic activities. A good program of

interscholastic activities will:

1. Help to form leagues which sponsor all sports of interest to schools of similar size in the same geographic location. The function of the league is to organize, plan, promote, and administer activities in an educationally sound manner.

2. Cover all participants with adequate and appropriate insurance, in case of injury.

3. Not establish scholastic eligibility standards for inter-school competition. It is not sound, educationally, to permit the use of standards in one part of the curriculum to determine whether a pupil may participate in another part of the curriculum.

4. Restrict pupils on an interscholastic team by not allowing them to play the same sport on an intramural or extramural basis.

5. Not be used as a substitute for class instruction in physical education. All pupils who are on interscholastic teams should still attend physical education classes.

6. Be an effectively organized and well-coordinated phase of the secondary-school curriculum, and an integrated and an integrated and balanced part of the total physical education program.

7. Receive a share of tax funds and school facilities, since it is an integral part of the education program.

8. Promote amateurism, rather than professionalism and commercialism.

9. Include a wide variety of activities during each

sports season, so that all pupils may participate.

10. Promote ethics and sportsmanship among the participants, spectators, and coaches.

11. Help to form togues which sponsor all sports of interest to schools of similar size in the same geographic location. The function of the league is to organize, plan, promote, and administer activities in an educationally sound manner.

12. Cover all participants with adequate and appropriate insurance, in case of injury.

13. Not establish scholastic eligibility standards for inter-school competition. It is not sound, educationally, to permit the use of standards in one part of the curriculum to determine whether a pupil may participate in another part of the curriculum.

14. Restrict pupils on an interscholastic team by not allowing them to play the same sport on an intramural or extramural basis.

15. Not be used as a substitute for class instruction in physical education. All pupils who are on interscholastic teams should still attend physical education classes.

Class Program: Situations and Analysis

First situation: Showering

Mr. Scott, the new Director of Physical Education for the Jamestown Public Schools, is alarmed to find that most pupils in the schools do not take showers after participating in physical activity. The high school physical education teachers complain that a 45 minute period is not long enough for the pupils to shower. The elementary schools have dressing-showering facilities but do not use the showers.

Questions

Why should pupils take showers? Is a 45 minute period enough time to include showering? At what grade level should showering be initiated? Should there be an administrative policy in regard to showering?

Analysis

Showering is recognized as an integral part of the health and physical education programs. If the programs of health teaching and health guidance are to be effective, and if personal health standards are to be maintained by individual pupils, the taking of a shower after physical activity is essential. It should be the responsibility of the school to facilitate this phase of the program by proper scheduling.

This is especially true in the elementary grades, where many of the physical education classes are scheduled for 25 to 30 minutes. This is not sufficient time for class activities plus dressing and showering. It is recommended that these periods be extended to 45 minutes so that pupils have adequate time to dress and shower properly. Many schools have their pupils shower by the third or fourth grade.

When schools initiate showering in these grades, there are usually fewer problems about it in the junior and senior high-school grades. Eight to twelve-year-old pupils are ready for showering and should not be denied the opportunity of establishing this desirable health practice. With these youngsters, the problem is not getting them into the shower, but getting them out of the shower. There should be an administrative policy in regard to showering.

This policy should be thoroughly discussed with the pupils by the physical education teachers so that it is understood by the pupils. In some school districts, it is a matter of educating not only the pupils but some of the parents as well.

Second Situation: Discipline by Another Teacher

In her first teaching assignment at Broadway Elementary School, Miss Means finds that one of the classes reporting for physical education lacks several pupils. After conferring with their classroom teacher, Miss Means finds that she kept the children in the classroom as a disciplinary measure because they misbehaved.

Questions

Should an elementary-school classroom teacher be able to keep pupils in the classroom as a disciplinary measure while other pupils in the same class are participating in scheduled physical education? What would be acceptable disciplinary measures for the classroom teacher to take? Should there be an administrative policy which determines how teachers should discipline pupils?

Analysis

It is not educationally sound for a classroom teacher to keep a pupil out of scheduled physical education. The elementary-grade pupil has great need for vigorous activity. At this age level, it is essential that all pupils receive instruction in the basic skills related to physical education. Disciplinary measures will vary with the type and extent of misbehavior of the pupil, but in no case should a pupil be removed from the physical-education program as a disciplinary measure. In order to make sure that all pupils are treated fairly and that individual teachers have guidance about disciplinary procedures, administrative policies should be established and made known to all teachers. Miss Means should check with the principal of the school to see if there are any such policies.

Third Situation The Ballet Dancer

Miss Jones, the girls' physical education teacher at Ontario High School, has received a telephone call from a mother who wants her daughter excused from physical education because she is taking ballet lessons. The mother thinks that her daughter is getting enough exercise and could better spend her time in study hall.

Questions

Does ballet make a contribution to a girl's body development? Is body development the only objective of the physical education program? Can the total objectives of physical education be met through ballet lessons?

Analysis

Balloet has definite value in the development of the total body. How ever, its primary contribution is to the development of the lower extremities. In order to develop the total body, it is necessary for pupils to participate in a variety of physical education activities–games gymnastics, and swimming. Body development makes a contribution to physical fitness and is the unique objective of physical education. However, there are other important objectives of the program, such as skills, knowledge, and social competence. Ballet contributes to the development of skills, knowledge, and social competence, but only in relation to this specific activity.

It makes little or no contribution to these objectives as they are related to the many activities that should be included in a good program of physical education. Miss Jones, in her conversation with the mother, should indicate the desirability of ballet lessons.

Her daughter's interest and skill in ballet will make her of great assistance to Miss Jones as a leader and demonstrator of rhythms and dance activities. It should also be mentioned to the parent that ballet dancing, for most people, does not have great carry-over value and that there are numerous other activities which pupils participate in which they will engage in later life.

Fourth Situation: the National Guard

Mr. Bennett, a high school physical education teacher, received a note from Mrs. Jones, who wants her boy excused from physical education because he is in the National Guard. What should be Mr. Bennett's reaction to this request?

Questions

Does participation in the National Guard contribute to the objectives of physical education? Are there laws requiring pupils to take physical education classes?

Analysis

Participation in the National Guard does make a limited contribution to the objectives of physical education, but its major emphasis is on military drill. This cannot possible replace the varied offerings of a good physical education program, which stresses physical, mental, emotional and social development through many different types of physical activities. A majority of the states have laws which require that physical education be taught in the public schools, legislation which was usually initiated because the public was concerned about the lack of physical fitness of men going into the armed forces.

Many military leaders have gone on record as indicating that drill is improved when the men have had physical education and that the greatest contribution the school can make is to make their students physically fit by means of a good physical education program.

9

FINANCIAL MANAGEMENT

In order for a program of education to be adequate, it is essential that a community have sufficient financial resources and be willing to spend them. Where such conditions exist a comprehensive instructional program and related services are usually provided. However, in school systems where funds are inadequate, instruction and services may be extremely limited or even nonexistent.

Physical education, including athletics, are adversely affected or may not be provided at all. Physical education and intramural activities usually suffer as a result of insufficient staff, supplies, and equipment, and inter-school athletics become dependent upon gate receipts.

Financial Management in Physical Education

An effective program of physical education requires one of the largest outlays in the educational budget. Such factors as facilities, personnel, supplies, and equipment contribute to the total cost.

Because of the great expense involved, it is essential that there be appropriate financial management to insure that funds are used in the most advantageous manner. There are a number of reasons why financial management is essential in the conduct of physical education programs, including; (1) to utilize funds in such a way as to provide for the best possible physical education program; (2) to make maximum use of factors such as facilities, personnel, supplies and equipment in achieving program objectives; (3) to avoid improper use and waste of funds; and (4) to involve all of the physical education staff in developing financial policies and procedures designed to give proper direction to the program.

Sources of Income for Public Education

Funds for public education come primarily from a variety of government sources, including local, state, and federal allocations. Local taxes and state aid usually make up the support. The financial responsibility for most public-school systems is undertaken by the local community, and the most common procedure for obtaining funds is through taxation.

The procedures by which local taxes are levied and bond issues circulated is specifically determined by law. In recent years, the states have assumed a larger share of the financial responsibility for supporting their educational programs. State aid is determined by the ability of the municipality to pay its educational expenses, according to a formula established by the state. State school funds are secured through tax procedures similar to those used in local communities.

Many states provide additional aid for improving such special school programs as vocational education, education for the physically, mentally, and emotionally handicapped pupils, and transportation of schoolchildren. Federal aid to education has also increased considerably, and communities with programs that adhere to specific requirements receive federal funds for education. Besides special types of educational programs, federal aid is given for school inches, vocational education, and the education of children of federal aid is given for school lunches, vocational education, and the education of children of federal employees. Other sources of income for financing local school programs of education are quite limited.

Some private foundations interested in supporting worthwhile educational activities have given grants to school systems for implementing educational programs. Gifts and donations from private organizations and individuals may also be sources of income.

The Budget for Interscholastic Athletics

The cost of conducting inter-school athletic activities should be supported by the board of education in the same way as other areas of the curriculum. Such a policy would reduce many of the problems currently associated with inter-school athletics and incorporate it as an educational activity within the total program of physical education. The law permitting boards of education to expend funds for the support of inter-school athletics varies in different states.

Some states have ruled that boards of education have no legal power to expend money for inter-school athletics since such activities are not a proper public-school activity within the scope of physical education as thew term is stated in the law. Other states have interpreted inter-school athletics as an integrals part of the physical education program, and their boards of education do have legal power to provide financial support for these activities. In situations where gate receipts, student athletic association funds, and donations provide the major source of revenue for the conduct of inter-school athletic activities, it is advisable to place such money under the supervision of the school district's business manager and make it part of the general school fund.

General school funds may be allocated to such activities as band, glee club, dramatics, and intramural and inter-school athletics. Each activity develops its budget and receives appropriate financial support through the general fund. Among the advantages of such a system are:

1. It enables the school administrator to have a composite picture of the general condition, financial and otherwise, of all the school activities.

2. It provides the possibility for a much more accurate audit of school activities funds than otherwise might be the case.

3. Responsibility for disbursement of all school funds may be delegated to one individual.

4. It is in harmony with the plan of having all school activities under the general supervision of an all-school committee.

5. By its nature, the play appeals to students and school patrons as being more businesslike.

6. The purposes for which expenditures are to be made may be more easily checked to ascertain if they are in accordance with authorization.

7. Local banking institutions usually will prefer a single school deposit account rather than separate ones for each school activity fund.

In some school districts it is the policy that each high school in the district have its own athletic budget, based upon the estimated receipts and expenditures for each activity.

In other school districts, particularly larger ones, it is often advantageous to allocate funds to each school on an equitable basis. Such a procedure is beneficial when the athletic funds of some schools are considerably greater than those of others. Other school districts have established policies whereby gate receipts become part of the general physical education budget and may be used to support all aspects of the physical education program.

Supplies and Equipment

Supplies are expendable materials that must be replaced quite often. Equipment is used over a period of years. Adequate supplies and equipment are essential in order to achieve program objectives, and they should be properly provided for in the budget. The selection of supplies and equipment should be based upon the needs of the local school.

The director, in cooperation with his physical education teachers and coaches, should select those items to be purchased. In large schools, a purchasing agent especially trained for such a responsibility usually does the purchasing. In small schools the director, teacher, or coach may do the buying, either directly or through the principal or business manager. The principles governing the policies and procedures used in the selection and care of physical education supplies and equipment should:

1. Enable the individual or agency purchasing materials to realize for every dollar expended the fullest possible return as measured by the number of units or periods of satisfactory use.

2. Be administered according to a plan which provides that all persons involved in the selection, use or care of equipment and supplies have clearly defined responsibilities and authority with respect to these functions.

3. Help assure each individual or group using the supplies the maximum benefit and enjoyment attainable from participation in the activities.

4. Enable individuals and groups to participate satisfactorily in activities that serve their basic needs and interests and that contribute to personal growth and development.

5. Help in the attainment of the goals and objectives of the program in which the equipment and supplies are used, such as physical development, recreation, or training in skills.

6. Encourage the development and use of new types of equipment that foster imaginative play and creative forms of activity.

7. Make possible during any given activity period optimum participation by all members of the group.]

8. Conform to widely accepted standards for the administration of athletic physical education, and recreation programs.

Budgeting for Physical Education and Athletics

The administration of a physical education program, including athletics, is an education enterprise. By necessity, however, it is also a business and must be conducted in a businesslike manner. This requires the determination of annual needs, income, and expenditures through the process of budgeting.

Budgeting is the development of a financial play based upon work to be done and services to be carried out. To be educationally sound, all expenditures listed in the budget should be specifically related to the achievement of program objectives. A budget is an organized statement of estimated receipts and expenditures.

It is an estimate of income and revenues for a one-year period, referred to as the fiscal year, which is not always the same as the school year. Although budgets are primarily concerned with a one-year period, they should also show long-term planning, indicating specific needs and costs, and provide for a well-planned program within the estimated income.

Budget Format

The format of the budget may vary. One budget might include a clear and concise introduction, designed to inform the school administration of the funds necessary to achieve the education goals of the program. This could be followed by a comprehensive overview of the budget, including general expenditures and proposed revenues. The next section might include a detailed presentation of estimated expenditures and receipts, organized so as to permit others to understand the budget and analyze its cost factors.

The final part of the budget could contain additional material intended to substantiate specific requests included in the budget. In most budgets, the items are classified into three general categories: (1) instruction; (2) capital outlay; and (3) maintenance and operation. An item such as coaches salaries would be included under instruction, a new swimming pool under capital outlay, and care of fields and grounds under maintenance and operation.

Financial Records

A detailed account of all monies expended for physical education is essential. The accounting system should include a record of all receipts and expenditures of funds. A periodic evaluation of the financial records should be conducted, to insure the proper management of funds. Some specific principles and policies concerning financial accounting include;

1. A system of accurate record keeping should be established and be uniform throughout the department.

2. The administrative head has the final responsibility for accountability for all equipment and supplies in his or her organization.

3. Departments should establish and enforce policies

covering loss, damage, theft, misappropriation, or destruction of equipment and supplies or other materials.

4. A system of policies should be developed that will guarantee the proper use and protection of all equipment and supplies within the department.

5. Accountability should demonstrate the close relationship that exists between equipment and supplies and the program objectives.

6. The discarding of equipment and supplies should take place only in accordance with established procedures and by authorized persons.

7. A meaningful procedure should be seta blushed for the proper distribution of all equipment and supplies.

8. A system of marking equipment and supplies as proof of ownership should be instituted.

9. Accurate inventories are an essential to proper financial accounting.

Purposes of A Budget

A sound budget will

1. Indicate where and when specific changes must be made to achieve certain objectives.

2. Indicate to the people of a school district what it costs in dollars and cents to provide a physical education program, including inter-school athletics.

3. Provide detailed information on physical education and athletic activities for which public funds are being used.

4. Protect the continuation of this program for a specified period of time.

5. Serve as a basis for determining the amount of money that must be obtained from local taxation.

6. Permit, with the approval of appropriate officials. The expenditure of funds for physical education.

7. Serve as a means of financial control.

Income and Expenditures

Most school physical education programs receive finances from the general school fund, gate receipts, and activity fees. The general school fund is the major source of financial support, but in some schools gate receipts are a significant factor in financing the program of physical education. Schools also obtain funds from activity fees, the cost of admission to extra-class activities such as athletic events, plays, and concerts. Expenditures for physical education usually involve capital outlays, such as for field renovations or a swimming pool; maintenance and operation outlays, such as for reconditioning uniforms and equipment, or for laundry service; and outlays for expendable equipment and supplies such as for gymnastic apparatus or balls and bats.

Preparing the Budget

There are several plans for preparing budgets in public schools. Often the budget is prepared by the school principal and eventually submitted to the chief school officer for approval by the board of education.

Or it may be developed by the chief school officer, who presents it to the principal for his comment and reaction. Sometimes the director of a specific school programs will develop a system-wide departmental budget and present it to the board of education through the chief school officer. The physical education budget should be prepared cooperatively by the department administrator and his staff. When the budget has been approved, it should provide guidance and direction for the financial operation and administration of the department. The budget should then be continually evaluated to ascertain its effectiveness in achieving educational objectives.

The Administration of the Budget

When the budget has been approved, it is usually the responsibility of the director of the department to the department to see that it is implemented. Before expending, funds, he should be informed of the amount of money remaining in each category. The budget should serve as a guide for efficient operation and be closely followed, in order to serve its serve its purpose.

Adopting the Budget

The school budget for physical education is usually approved initially by the principal; then, if the school system has such a person, by the chief school officer; and finally, by the board of adduction. A considerable amount of preparation should go into the final draft of the budget so that only minor changes are required for its adoption by the board of education.

All financial requests should be educationally sound, and appropriate individuals and groups should be informed of the content of the budget before it is submitted. Such procedures tend to reduce difficulties when the budget is presented for adoption.

Budget Situations and Analysis

First Situation: Laundry Equipment

Mr. Johnson, the director of health, physical education and recreation at Park Ridge Central Schools, has requested that a laundry unit be included in the plans for the new high school.

Dr. Benson, the superintendent of schools, believes it would be too expensive and is not necessary. What reasons should Mr. Johnson present in attempting to show the superintendent the benefits of a school laundry?

Questions

How much space is required to house a school laundry? Does a school laundry save money for a school district? What necessary services can a school laundry provide? In addition to saving money, what additional beneficial benefits does a school laundry provide?

Analysis

In planning new facilities, there is always concern about the space needed for the various areas of an educational program. It is a misconception that school laundries require considerable space.

It is possible for smaller schools to have adequate laundry facilities in a room 20 by 20 feet. In both of these rooms there will be adequate space for the laundry tray, washer-extractor, tumbler, and storage bins or shelves. A considerable amount of money can be saved when a school district has its own laundry because; (1)

renderable items are lass costly than items that are dry cleaned; (2) laundry items are kept in the school, with less loss; (3) and laundry items last longer because the school can control the laundering procedures.

It has been the experience of schools with their own laundries that they have saved enough money in one year to pay for the equipment. In addition to the laundering of towels and uniforms in physical education and athletics, a school laundry can serve the homemaking program and cafeteria, for example. Often there are emergencies or exceptional demands that are more adequately met when a school has its own laundry.

One of the greatest benefits that a school laundry provides is insuring that all pupils will have a clean uniform and towel when they are participating in physical education and athletics. This will help all pupils maintain desirable health practices.

Second situation: falling Gate Receipts

Melverne High School had championship athletic teams for a number of years. Part of the funds obtained from gate receipts have been used to purchase equipment and supplies for the physical education program. For the past three years their teams have won only a few games and sufficient funds are not available to purchase the equipment and supplies needed for physical education class instruction. What steps should be taken to improve this situation?

Questions

Should physical education class instruction be supported by funds from interscholastic contests? Should interscholastic athletics be supported by the gate receipts of games? Should the interscholastic team that has the greatest gate receipts receive most of the athletic budget?

Analysis

Physical education classes should be supported by funds from the regular school budget just as other subjects are. One part of the curriculum should not have to depend upon the success of another for financial support. Since physical education classes contribute to the education of every pupil, they should be included in each school budget.

How much and what types of equipment, supplies, and popularity are purchased for the physical education class-instruction program should not depend upon the success of any athletic team. When competitive athletics are conducted in a desirable way, they can make a significant contribution to the education curriculum.

Since interscholastic athletics are generally recognized as an integral part of the physical education program, they should be financially supported by funds of the board of education in the same way as other areas of the education curriculum. Where it is necessary to depend upon paid admissions for interscholastic contests, there will be a reflection of the public rather than the educational point of view. If athletics are ever going to reflect the views of education and not of the public, they must be independently financed. In situations where gate receipts support all or part of the interscholastic program, funds should nevertheless be allocated to each athletic team on an equitable basis.

The sport that receives the most in gate receipts

should not necessarily receive the most funds. Other factors should be considered, such as the number of pupils served, the cost of supplies and equipment, and the educational value of each activity.

Third Situation: Unobligated Equipment

The budgeted allocation for physical education supplies and equipment has been expended. Funds were not available to purchase a balance beam and vaulting box for use in gymnastics. The physical education staff at How Junior High School has obtained the cooperation of the industrial-arts department to construct these pieces of apparatus.

Questions

Are the balance beam and vaulting box necessary for teaching a broad program of gymnastics? Are there other means of getting funds for the apparatus? Should the industrial-arts department construct gymnasium apparatus?

Analysis

It is necessary to have several different pieces of apparatus in order to teach a broad program of gymnastics. The balance beam and the vaulting tax are recognized as essential pieces of equipment in this aspect of the physical education program. The value of the balance beam is that it provides opportunities for pupils to develop coordination, concentration, balance, and dexterity.

The vaulting box is probably the most natural and appealing to most pupils because running and leaping are fundamental motor skills. It is probably the most versatile vaulting apparatus because it can be used lengthwise, sidewise, or diagonally, and its height can be easily adjusted to meet the needs of various pupils. There are several ways of obtaining monies for the purchase of necessary gymnasium apparatus, depending upon the school and community.

In some school districts where there are active Parent-Teachers Associations, funds are given to the schools for the purchase of such equipment. Individual citizens who are interested in the physical education program sometimes donate money specifically for it.

Commercial and industrial businesses may sometimes make contributions to schools for the purchase of necessary teaching supplies and equipment. In communities where there are active service clubs, these often make contributions to school districts when there is a need.

The physical education staff at Hole Junior High School Should confer with their principal to see if any funds are available from such sources. In school districts where there are adequate industrial-arts departments it may be possible to construct gymnasium apparatus that would meet manufacturers specifications. When using such e equipment, the staff should test it thoroughly before allowing pupils to use it. However, it is more desirable to purchase gymnasium apparatus from a recognized equipment company whose materials have been tested and whose products meet specific safety standards.

Fourth Situation: A Trampoline

Each year Mr. Grover and Miss Stuart, the physical

education teachers at Known Elementary School, have includes a trampoline as one of the items in their budget request. Mr. Green, the principal, has refused to approve this budget item because he believes that it is too expensive and dangerous, and that pupils would receive limited use from it.

Miss Stuart and Mr. Grover have arranged to meet with the principal to discuss the situation.

Questions

Is a trampoline a desirable piece of apparatus for elementary-school physical education classes? Who should make the final decision for approving items in the physical education budget?

Analysis

The trampoline is a desirable piece of apparatus for elementary grade pupils because it develops timing, coordination, a sense of balance, and body control. Although there is limited evidence that certain elements of danger are involved in trampoline, there is no conclusive evidence to show that this piece of equipment is undesirable. Most of the research has been done with high-school and college students, and there is little evidence to show that it is not desirable form elementary grade pupils.

It is no more dangerous than other pieces of apparatus in the elementary-school gymnasium if proper instruction is provided and safety procedures are followed. It is true that usually only one pupil can use the trampoline at a time. However, the benefits gained from this piece of apparatus many not be obtainable on any other. For example, on no other piece of equipment can a pupil learn to control his body in the air as well as he can on a trampoline. The cost of the trampoline is greater than most other pieces of apparatus, but its unique value justifies its expense.

The final decision for approving items in the physical education budget should rest with Mr. Green, the principal. However, since Miss Stuart and Mr. Grover are the educational specialists in this area, they should be consulted. In their conference with Mr. Green, the physical education teachers should present justification for their request of the trampoline.

Fifth Situation: Supplies and Equipment

The physical education staff at the new Glenville Elementary School has been allocated a specific amount of money for supplies and equipment. In order to provide the best program possible within the budget allocation, what type and amount of supplies should be purchased by the physical education staff?

Questions

Is it possible to conduct a satisfactory program of physical education with little or no supplies or equipment? What priorities should be considered when purchasing supplies and equipment? What effect does available storage space have on the purchase of supplies and equipment? What effect does the number of pupils have on the purchase of supplies and equipment?

Analysis

Although a few physical education activities can be taught without some supplies and equipment, it is generally believed that in order to conduct a satisfactory program it is necessary to have a sufficient number and variety of supplies and equipment.

The physical education staff should determine whether the present supplies and equipment are adequate for the program. If there is a shortage of materials, priority should be given to purchasing necessary supplies and equipment for activities which presently are being taught. There should be sufficient storage space for all indoor and outdoor supplies and equipment to insure its being kept in a good and safe condition.

If there are insufficient areas for storage, it may be necessary to limit the type and amount of supplies and equipment until adequate space is obtained. When there is a limited area for storage, first consideration should be given to purchasing supplies and equipment that require little or no storage space. Such pieces of apparatus as ropes and rings require no special storage space, while a trampoline and parallel bars require considerable space. The number of pupils who use the supplies and equipment will help determine the amount needed.

This will also determine the type purchased in order to permit maximum participation. When all pupils participate, the individual pupil's needs and interests are met and a contribution is made to his personal growth and development.

10

CONCEPT OF PHYSICAL EDUCATION

Physical education in the nineteenth century presents a dismal Picture of drill masters, studs and superannuated army gymnasts who knew very little of modified Swedish gymnastics and nothing more than what the army had taught them for the conditioning of uncultured adult recruits.

No serious effort was made either by the Government or the educational authorities to the question of health, efficiency and harmonious development of the whole man

Birth of Physical Education on Our Soil

With the dawn of the twentieth century, the first rays of light shone upon this continent to enlighten people of the importance of physical fitness and a scientific physical education. It was the YMCAs in India which played a major role in spreading the new concept. It goes to the credit of America which produced great physical educational missionaries and the United Kingdom which sent great educationists to India.

Many leaders trained at the International College of Physical Education of YMCA at Springfield USA, have done pioneering work in the field of physical education in India and other countries in the East.

An Institution for Physical Education

With the arrival in 1908 of Dr. Henry Gray as the first Physical Director of the National YMCA at Calcutta a new emphasis was given to physical education. Through lectures, demonstrations and through a programma of physical training, games and sports in the various YMCAs in India, Dr. Gray and his associates created a new interest in Physical Education on modern lines. Later Dr. A.G. Noehren as the National Physical Director of YMCAs of India, continued the work of Dr. Gray. A young American, H.C. Buck, then doing physical education work at Wichita, Kansas, came to India in September 1918 to take service as Physical Director at the Central YMCA, Madras.

He studied the existing situation in the country, felt the great need for training leadership in the field, and established a School of Physical Education in the year 1920 at Madras, which has today blossomed into the YMCA College of Physical Education.

From H.C. Buck's Physical Education

H.C. Buck found in physical education a field where all the races and creeds of the world can come together and meet in the worship of those qualities of love and forgiveness, beauty and splendor, truth and justice, equanimity and kindness which are essential for a good life.

In 1919, he started as a humble worker as Physical Director and co-worker with Dr. Noehren at the Central YMCA Madras, and was soon able to indicate in his statements orderliness, discipline, respect for rules and a host of other qualities essential for sportsmen and a good citizen. Buck's vision, his faith and optimism, his tenacity of purpose, his untiring zeal, his geniality and inherent goodness, his limitless industry and immense capacity for leadership, were the materials which contributed to the stately steel frame of that edifice which he raised and endowed with strength and richness to the traditions it created and treasured for the betterment of the youth of India. Till about the twenties physical education was unknown to this country and its educational system.

Educationists did indeed believe in the old adage mens Sana in Corpoere Sano but all that was done in schools to put that saying into practice was to give the pupils an occasional hour of drill in the week and, where convenience permitted and facilities could be had without trouble, a team of star players in football or badminton was trained.

The instructors were ignorant and ill-paid. There was no attempt to provide for and much less to teach games to pupils.

Drill was done only outside the school hours and even that was more or less unrelated to the school curriculum. The drill master was accordingly the Cinderella of the school staff and could often be bought off or placated without difficulty by influential pupils.

The drill master often used language and adopted methods which we should associate with the back streets of olden days. Even the check that drill masters wore spoke of their outlook and attitude, for when they did not choose to wear their old army uniforms, they generally donned the familiar but grotesque dress peculiar to circus ringmasters of games.

These drill masters knew little or nothing, nor were they interested. Further, where an attempt was made to provide facilities for play they were left to the care of someone among the teachers of the three as and the drill masters could hardly poach upon the preserves of honorary superintendents of games. Despite the lack of any general provision for games for all pupils, headmasters and principals, book-inspired and anxious to emulate British examples, talked glibly of the many virtues of team games and the benefits accruing from pupil participation in sports. In fact, evert in this country it was a common belief that the Battle of Waterloo was won on the polyphagies of Eton and Harrow. No serious effort was, however, made to give thought to the questions of the health and efficiency of the school child.

This cannot be considered strange in a country where not only education but even administration has tended till quite recently to function according to the convenience of the rulers, whose main aim naturally centrad directly or indirectly on their own interests, rather than on the health and progress of the people.

Aim & Physical Education

Physical education should aim to provide skilled leadership, adequate facilities and ample time for affording full opportunity for inaividuals and groups to participate in situations that are physical wholesome, mentally stimulating and satisfying and socially sound. This implies a thorough understanding of the nature and needs of the participants and the implementation of a programme utilising activities and facilities catering to these interests and needs.

Objectives

1. Increase in strength and neuro-muscular control.

2. Acquisition of skills, habits and attitudes in a variety of physical activities which will contribute to wholesome and enjoyable juicer pursuits.

3. Protection and improvement of health and the development of organic fitness.

4. Development of desirable social attitudes and standards of conduct.

Interpretation

Physical education is that part of the general education programme which is concerned with the growth development and education of children through the medium of muscular activities. It is education of the whole child by means of physical activities. They are so selected and conducted as to influence every aspect of the child's life physically, mentally, emotionality and morally.

Some of the reasons why physical education and scientifically trained physical educators are necessary in India are the following:

1. Child marriage.

2. General disinclination to exercises which develop hardihood.

3. Need of training in high ideals of sportsmanship.

4. Ignorance of sex matters.

5. Widespread use of drugs and other forms of addiction.

6. Lack of attention to sanitation.

7. Improper diet.

N.K. Mia says in his article: Buch and the Y.M.C.A. College of Physical Education.

But in the last analysis, if India in to be saved, she must save herself. We cannot for ever bear all her burdens. India and Indians are best understood by her own people.

This being so it seems only proper that this programme of physical regeneration should be carried on by the sons of India. Our attempt at depending upon foreign Physical Directors to do the job has been futile and the solution lies in training indigenous leadership.

The trying climate and the constantly changing personnel along with other factors convinces that if someone give himself to the work of the necessity of training men to carry on the work among them and among their own people. Weakened help from America which has the money, the man power and the experience. All these are needed in helping India to help herself, and our prayer is that individuals in America may be made to see this opportunity to serve each according to his talents.

In spite of an abundance of acceptable interpretations and advice from authoritative writers and speakers, there is still a tendency to cling to readmitted methods and systems of physical education.

Therefore, whether physical education has any place

in the present social order and whether it can contribute anything of value to modern life, will depend entirely upon our intention to continue to cling tenaciously to the traditionally formalised and standardised schemes of physical education based on some artificial system of exercises.

We may assume at the outset that in any educational procedure the sensible thing to do is to be guided by the facts obtained from a study of human nature and to build up our programme in the light of the facts so discovered.

It is education of the whole man through the medium of physical activities. As such, the activities should be carefully selected and conducted. Physical education in the past has suffered from the same defects as general education. There has been too great a tendency to follow the line of least resistance and to fit individuals and groups to pre-conceived schemes of work instead of fitting the programme to the interests and needs of work instead of fitting the programme to the interests and needs of those being educated.

Such misguided procedures are not likely to bring the desired results. Both education and physical education must provide experiences that are life like and which will produce personalities capable of adjusting to the present-day social order. A study of the history of physical education reveals that much valuable time has been wasted in squabbles over the merits and demerits of various systems. The introduction of all sorts of arts has only frustrated the school and college students who have almost rebelled against the system. As N.K. Mia says, "These young men were to get themselves equipped for the great task that lay ahead- the vision of a new India with strong men and healthy and happy women. It was a venture of faith and great challenge worthy of the best.

Research, Education and Physical Education

A variety of research fronts established in the industrial sphere were the causative factor for the industrial revolution that has taken place.

In the field of humanities or the human sciences, research has contributed new frontiers of knowledge. This is particularly true in the area of medicine, engineering, sociology and psychology. In India physical education is a growing field and if it is to be made scientific and comparable with other advanced fields such as medicine, engineering, science, agriculture, etc., it is essential that more and more research should be undertaken in this field under the available conditions.

There is no doubt that numerous research studies can be carried out on the playfully itself. Yet adequate and appropriate space is needed where sophisticated instruments can be installed and research studies conducted under controlled conditions. Education is usually regarded as acquisition of knowledge.

It is defined as the art of making available to each generation the organised knowledge of the past. It also involves the aggregate of all the processes by means of which a person develops abilities, attitudes and other forms of positive faculties in the society in which he lives.

More than acquiring knowledge, it cultivates a cluster of attitudes and skills. The ability to think independently and clearly is of major importance. Education thus becomes a means to an end, not an end by itself. It is with a view to developing the overall personality of youth that physical education has been made a part of general education. Education is control of the development of knowledge and formation of the whole structure of man.

Physical education is now being recognised as a part of total education as a phase of general education and as a way of real education.

Of all animals, man has been the most successful in the constant struggle against the environment. Even though he cannot run as fast as some quadrupeds, swim like dolphins, climb like apes, fly as birds do, he has been the only creature capable of defying the forces of gravity and reaching the realms of outer space.

The one factor that has enabled him to accomplish this feat is his ingenuity and intelligence in understanding the stories of nature. Man has consistently striven to run faster, jump higher, throw farther and have greater speed, power and strength. Physical education and sports alter the very essence of life.

They shape social and human needs, bring greater good will and closer contact in the comity of nations. Physical education is extremely essential for helping to remove he differences between mental and physical work. The study of man and motion is a complex task. We cannot comprehend man as a whole. We know him as the macrocosm of distinct parts and the cream of creation. Today research enjoys a prestigious place in physical education and coaching programmes.

The scholar should be fully aware of the purposes to be served by the research which he undertakes, whether it is applied or pure research.

He should be able to conduct the research in an objective way. He should be able to communicate his experience, observations and findings in a cogent and clear-cut manner. Then only can the scholar justify his placement. The research worker's mission should be to conduct a research programme which will benefit the discipline of area selected by him. The ability to analyst critically is a necessary attribute of a successful researcher.

The problems the scholars face are:

a) Problems related to the sources of information; reference books are the only commonly available ais research; equipment and other facilities have not been strengthened to a satisfactory extent;

b) Problems related to time: in the majority of cases, the completion of research takes at least four years;

c) there is more confusion in selection the topic than in selection the director.

(d) the majority of scholars feel that their research has no practical application, but just serves as a stop-gap arrangement.

General

Even ancient man, knowingly or unknowingly, underwent vigorous physical exertion. Physical activity was part and parcel of his every endeavour. The modern man, even after relishing and relishing the higher values and fruits of physical education, unfortunately neglects physical activity. Trained leaders of physical education have failed in advocating or defining the concept of physical education. They have defined it in terms of sports and games. Thus, the tremendous effects and sacred values of physical education have been reduced to the very minimum. In the recent times, the concept of physical education has been accorded due importance, attention and recognition.

Experts from various quarters have started patronising the onetime neglected field on releasing its merits. The old-timers are of the opinion that physical education was meant for those who were gifted with physical strength and prowess.

Such misconceptions are no more valid. Now the trend is that physical education is a must for every human being at all age levels for a complete life. It has wonderful potentialities and tremendous a virtues to give to every man under the sun. Very many constructive literary works have come out from time to time to time on themes like specialised and specific games, its history and contribution to health and recreation, growth and development of physical education and allied fields.

But to our surprise, it has still not been considered as an academic subject in the true sense and remains simply either an extra curricular or literature on the subject. It is a healthy indication if a discipline grows in its structure, dimension and application.

The expansion of physical education is quite possible

if it draws concepts and laws from other allied branches of knowledge. Physical education has enriched its content and scope by deriving sports from medicine and yoga from philosophy. Apart from such induction of allied knowledge, there have been developments of the principal concepts improvements of the pattern of games, in the design of equipments, playing conditions, techniques of coaching methods, methodical organisation and administration, the use of tests and measurements in physical education, etc. This remarkable improvement has helped those who are directly or indirectly involved in the field of physical education.

Researches in physical education conducted all over the world in the past years, have provided highly beneficial ideas and novel advantages. In the hoary past, all over the world exercises were mostly associated with the rigorous training of the military services. Man and his actions should be in accordance with mother nature for a healthy and happy existence. Physical educations is largely advocated in Western countries to promote the well-being of the population at large, right from the young stage for effective functioning of the human internal systems as well as effective functioning of the body and for efficient performance on the sports arena.

The basic principles of natural movement are consistent with that of general education and were formulated as a direct response to the recognition that our older practices and ideas in physical education were consistent with the modern philosophy of education.

Philosophy and physical education are as interrelated and inseparable as two sides of the same coin and they play a dynamic role in shaping the life of an individual or an individual of in a group. The spectacular professional career of a physical educator enlivens and enlightens the mentality and mode of action of the young students in the high schools and colleges, particularly in the matters relating to sports career. The impact of concrete and compact concepts of physical education eventually makes a break through in their outlook and day to day life. As the first phase the physical educators are expected to develop mental attitudes and skills and undergo hardship, stress and strain besides sacrifices.

The physical educators should take the initiative to render the service of uplifting the profession and the young student community at large, bearing in mind the following key points: code of behavior, professional attitude, philosophy of the profession, professional attitude, philosophy of the profession professional commitment and job satisfaction which are to be given due stress in the course of his accomplishments. The physical educator has to march a long way for transforming his personal and technical personality for the cause of the cherished field of physical education, as well as the positive transformation of the domain of physical education.

The physical educator has been entrusted with a great mission of teaching for the betterment of his students and his profession. However he has not been provided with the ideal type of professional training. He does not enjoy the privilege of having well-defined clients to render service to. His clients are in a way vague, will nile and general in nature. The clients do not come forward with specific and clear-cut defects, deficiencies and problems. In spite of these drawbacks most of the physical educators do spot out the innate and latent talents of the students and inspire and encourage them to specialist in specific areas. They enrich the trainees or students by feeding appropriate theoretical knowledge as well.

Play and Child

In the modern world, the objective of education is the development of intellectual skills like thinking, planning and imagination, achieving social skills like competition, cooperative feelings, endurance and emotional maturity besides psychomotor skills and abilities like grip, coordination, strength, etc. In this respect, the educational objectives and processes have a great impact on physical education. The scholarly learning which the students acquire in the classroom can have tremendous relevance and impact in the playground.

The quantum and quality of learning differ from age to age. As the child grows physically and mentally, he exhibits variations of learning level. In the initial stage, educational perspective is conglomerating of certain measures like action and rest, success and failure, nervousness and fear of facing competition. The child may not be fully aware of the competition and may not be equipped to participate in serious competitions in all aspects.

A fully grown student is mature enough to make himself ready and fit for participation in physical activities and to analyses his own performance for further rectification and improvement. A seasoned sportsman is far advanced in playing techniques, anticipating the type and nature of performance of the opponents and entering into the playful in a well-prepared manner to face fatefully the opposing sportsman. There is every possibility for a shrewd and strategic sportsman to transform and apply the classroom knowledge and fruitful experience in the playfully and also throughout his lifetime, in whichever walk of life he may choose. Ultimately it is quite obvious that the educational perspective of physical education programmes does help a student to lead a meaningful and disciplined life with the right convictions and attitude. It is quite clear that every child, when entering the play-field considers himself, consciously or unconsciously, as a separate and individualised entity during every moment of play.

The child is demonstrating his actions with the force of his physiological and academic background. The personality traits and the knowledge learn in the classroom are reflected in his play. Every sportsman needs a basic or minimum level of literacy and communicative skills because physical activity is controlled by written and verbal commands. Nowadays, a sportsman has to operate or use sophisticated sports equipment or gadgets for advanced training and better performance.

So, it becomes all the more important for personnel involved in games and sports, chiefly for the sportsman, to have the unique personality, basic educational status and novel scientific ideas to explore and exploit new methods and openings in the vista of physical education and sports. A child is exposed to several kinds of experiences, many situations and opportunities which mould his thinking,. Imagination and deeds.

In the educational institutions, the educational perspective helps him to interpret and understand the experiences and outcomes of the play-fields. The attitude, and action of a student should be analyses in totality, taking into consideration both classroom performance and playground achievements.

The psychological disorders such as dejection and frustration which affect students may be due to the direct or indirect effect of the interaction of the pleasant or unpleasant experiences that the students may have undergone. The physical educator should take the utmost care to diagnose these correctly and extend guidance and counselling. The partial and incomplete approach by the physical educator may impair the physical and psychological constitution of the child. The crux of the problem is that the classroom teachers do not have any active hand in the practical affairs of the field and, likewise, the physical educators do not take part in the classroom teaching and other curricular programmes.

So there is a yawning gap between these two. They must plan an effective solution to bridge the gap so that the students acquire harmonious, healthy and rich knowledge from the teachers of both general education and physical education. Physical education is an unparalleled domain, because it helps students to reap maximum benefits.

There have to be certain pre-conditions like positive biological endowment, creating positive educational goals and appropriate opportunities for the child to interact with the school in a positive manner and to be conscious of the educational outcome of such interaction.

The learning of the child is dependent upon nature, environment, facilities of the educational institution, etc. There are noticeable differences between a child from a school with all the facilities and the one from a school which is not equipped with the necessary amenities and facilities. A child who emerges out of a rural school will lag behind the other schlieren in almost every aspect. Moreover, the invaluable and formative ideas and experiences that a child learns from the inter-school and intra-school competitions also differ from situation to situation. Traits such as presence of mind, intelligence, performance in the field surely will have an impact and carry-over value and will definitely have a say in their later life. The play-field can be described as a miniature classroom where many of the educational processes are going on to help them to achieve skills, performance and character traits through play interaction. Sports and games provide numerous opportunities for the players to strike up interaction between various personalities.

A player has to move with the manager, coach, referee, captains, player has to move with the manager, coach, referee, captains, playmates, etc. This interaction may help or hinder the purpose of physical development and educational growth. The physical educators and coaches must bear in mind factors such as individual difference and the interaction between the player and the physical activity.

They only can they render service effectively. The individual differences may be of many kinds-physiological social, psychological, physical and educational, capacities, resources and limitations that an individual exhibits from time to time. The play-field is an open laboratory which does not have physical boundaries. Here the sky is the limit. The playground activities inspire many young ones to fight in a healthy manner in order to achieve victory.

This correlates the educational goal with that of physical education. The open-field classroom help young children to adapt themselves to failures, and frustration, victory and defeat, individual honor and group triumph and emotional ups and downs. The play-field can reject players push them to its boundaries and make them wish to lose. It also, at times, depresses, exhilarates and stimulates. It sorts out the individual players according to their capacity, performance and status. The educational aim of play at a given moment may be to teach the rules of the games, to teach the physical activities, etc. The educative atmosphere in the institutions may create a spirit of competition and cooperation, domination, democracy, stimulation and depression. The participants may not have the same mental calibre or interest in physical events. The intensity of seriousness, and the degree of genuine interest on the part of the participant sportsman may vary according to the personality and nature of the sportsman. It is high time that we plan meticulously the various ways to learn the physical activities in a scientific manner, like our predecessors, so that we can hand over a standardised knowledge to our younger generation.

Hence physical activities become sufficiently educational, if they develop this capacity to inherit from our predecessors and extend to our progeny. The continuous emphasis of the moral approach and attempt of the physical education policy will bring about solid progress. Physical education helps to provide this continuity in action and thought. The learning that is taking place inside the classroom should be continued and carried on outside also.

No doubt, the playground is the agency and medium that offers continuity to education. There are other agencies such as the family, neighbourhood, professional pilocarpus, government, mass media, to give continuity and perpetuate the career of people by inducting them into the educational sphere. The physical educator and coach should select appropriate physical activities, and ancillary equipment that will improve the spirit of commitment of the professional.

The general pattern of sport and games and all the inherent programmes have been structured from the sphere of general education. The policies and programmes of physical education should always be in accordance with general education policies. The school and the playground play a predominant role in the formation of a strong personality in children as they spend the major part of the day time in schools.

Physical Education

Physical movements are a biological necessity. Physical education has devised organised games and sports in systematic way within the educational institutions. A student learns a lot when he takes part in any event. He understands the nature and inherent techniques of a phenomenon by the trial and error methods, thereby mastering the do's and don'ts of a particular area.

Thus an individual is facilitated in having a wide scope of learning by himself through the medium of physical activities in an educational atmosphere. This may be called the self-analysis function of scientific physical activity. The educational values of physical education can be acquired in the open classroom, i.e., the playground where the instructor conducts various types of activities which provide ample opportunities for character development, play-interaction, shouldering responsibility and practising the art acquired before. The participation in the field activities directs and educates the students. The classroom and the playground are the twin places where the students can experiment with their innate talents in order to evaluate themselves and put into practice their worth.

There is the possibility also to compensate by performing well in the field in case anybody is weak in classroom achievements, or a student may even retain the same high position in both the places. Physical education is a superb field wherein ample opportunities are created for the development of complete personality through coordinated physical activities.

The unique feature of physical education programmes is that participants willingly engage themselves without any kind of hesitation, inhibitions and reservations. No doubt, other academic and social media of the school like the curriculum, classroom, administrative machinery and examination system also play a significant role in the formation of wholesome personality, but physical education contributes a vital part of the total general education pattern. Physical Education had to pass through a number of ordeals, and tribulations to its achieve present prestigious status.

Physical education programmes were considered to be the extracurricular and evening-hour recreational activities in those days, whereas it enjoys an enviable position now because researches and innovations were made in curricula and in implementation of the designed activities. Moreover, it has been proved that there is a direct relationship between scholastic standing and the physical performance in the field. So also, the physical educators in schools and colleges now enjoy honer and professional status and they are on the faculty councils and university committees.

This clearly indicates that physical education has been recognised and universally accepted as being on par with other departments of knowledge. Physical education has many wings such as athletics associations, amateur associations, professional units, coaching centres, etc., in which specialised personnel are working hard for the improvement of the specific purposes. It is a healthy sign if there is meaningful and coordinated integration for the overall prosperity of the entire field. The question arises: Is there integration and coordination between general education and physical education? Undoubtedly, a congenial atmosphere has been established between physical education and general education. Moreover, the wide gap has been almost bridged. In schools and colleges, physical education programmes have been made compulsory for all the students and thus a mutual interdependence between them has been well established.

It is not wrong to say that physical education and general education are inseparable. The physical educators of today have been entrusted with greater responsibilities in keeping with the changed curriculum. In the past, physical education was thought of as improving the physique, strength and motor skills, whereas it now aims at improving the overall personality of a man. It is a healthy sing that physical education has been accorded the right place which has enlarged its aims and objectives. It is the moral duty of the whole physical education machinery to tone itself so as to make a breakthrough in this field. The chief aim of physical education is to create ideal opportunities for young students at various levels to acquire the true and all round perfection and development in every aspect.

The main objectives of the multifarious programmes of physical education is to produce responsible and rational citizens who act wisely throughout their lives. We have not yet succeeded in this particular aspect and angle. There is no shadow of doubt that we have to go a long way in order to realise the goals of physical education.

Education

Education principles are patterned in such a way that the students in schools and colleges are moulded into complete personalities by means of guided participation. The child has to be looked after and nourished systematically and scientifically by the teachers at various levels.

The medium for this sacred task is the well-designed and balanced physical education programmes. According to scientific educational techniques, the teachers should pick out the positive as well as negative aspects of the students under them, and do their best to analyse and synthesis the psychological and emotional demands of the students. Guidance and counselling can be rendered to the students for their betterment by the physical education teachers.

The students should be trained to transfer the skills or talents acquired to the other domains in which they may involve themselves in later phases of life. It is quite appropriate to have strict and stipulated norms of physical efficiency for admitting the students into educational impractical in day-to-day life.

This sound rigid, unconventional and impractical in day to day life. This pattern of admission will hold good in due course and help to realise the true aims and objectives of physical Education and make us reap the real fruits there of. We can then produce totally developed personalities more easily. Educational commentators, academic experts and other critics question the contributory role of physical education and its related subjects in vogue in producing a substantial positive effect in the mind and beau voir of the people. If it does not prove to be good, competitive sports and games can be brought to a halt, which are just a national waste. It is more purposeful if we plan meticulously for mass participation, group involvement, and mass level fitness and health programmes along with great emphasis on recreational activities which are highly conducive in making a strong, solid, cultured and healthy society. Education has been defined as a change, modification of an adjustment on the part of the student as a result of fruitful experiments and experiences.

Physical education is called an integral part of the total educational process which combines the physical, social and psychological aspects of man's life, through well-directed physical activities. There are other sciences like physics and medicine which have enriched the content of physical education. The educational principles chiefly aim at producing well bread and well-balanced children who will adjust with and adapt to the real problems in their future life-style.

The planned programme should be congenial to the philosophy and goal of the individuals, groups or communities for whom it is designed. Meaningless theory and unsuitable activities should be eliminated because they fail to satisfy and fulfil the requirements of the pupils for personality growth.

The original thrust of the educational policy is aimed at the improvement of academic standards thereby enriching the intellectual spheres of the students. This concept, when put into practice in the past, did not come up to expectations for reasons like imbalanced character development and other serious handicaps which could have been avoided, to a great extent, if combined efforts had been undertaken to influence the young children as well as college going students in the right academic perspectives. The total development of the individual is of prime importance.

The experts in the field of education must find out ideal means, methods and agencies through which the total development can be achieved in practical life. The various physical activities are the media, which are considered as educational objectives and means to achieve the total objective of integrated development. The physical education policies and programmes, along with education-oriented approaches, will successfully create the required personality traits among the students.

It is high time that we totally discard the traditional concepts of phvsical education which develop mutual indifference, confrontation and isolation between education and physical education. Education with its dynamic nature and thrust towards improvement should concentrate on imparting valuable knowledge in health education, movement education, recreation, physical education, vocational education, fine arts, etc., to the children at early period of their lives. If we look back to the concepts of education of the ancient Spartan government, we come to know that the aim of education was to produce men of action and individual physical excellence so that the individual could be put to the service of the country especially in times of emergency and war. In those days, human power was chiefly utilised for military purposes as countries were waging wars for survival constantly, and to establish their supremacy over the others.

Apparently the idea was to keep the citizens physically sound so as to live life to the fullest and they sought wholesome activities that aimed at harmonious development of the body. In short, the whole educational pattern was to channelise the youth towards military objectives. However, the aim today is to develop the total personality of man for a better life. These above said educational objectives can be achieved provided the programmes of physical education fit into the educational perspective of the total system.

The dynamic operations of the educational system should be well understood by men who are entrusted with the work of gearing up the administrative machinery of physical education. The physical educators should take utmost care that they must not overemphasize the importance of the physical aspects of the game situation and the educational values should also be developed among the students for fuller growth.

Students may become completely balanced and grown up in every aspect only if both the values are developed hand in hand. As a matter of fact, physical education has not been given educational orientation because the recreational aspects enjoy more importance than the educational aspects. The formulation of the various physical activities must be done taking the educational principles into account.

The general education pattern must yield to certain positive changes and transformation in its structure and policy for this purpose. The key points such as the developmental characteristics of students, the principle of correlation between academic subjects and physical activities, the principle of student-teacher ratio, etc., should be given due place in the physical education curriculum. The sole purpose of physical activities should be the fulfillment of the higher values of general education.

Inter-discipline Relationship

No nascent discipline is rich in its structure and content. It has to grow with time. The experiments and research conducted explore the possibilities for further growth and enrichment. In this process, it has to make collaborative work with other disciplines from which concepts and professional formulae can be borrowed for its enlargement and application.

The interdisciplinary sharing of ideas and of joint efforts are applicable to any profession. Physical education is not an exception because if it acts in isolation its scope and growth are adversely affected. Some sort of mutual analysis and collaborative research work will therefore help to enrich the profession substantially. The field of physical education is ever, growing in all aspects.

It is in the process of enriching its major principles and premises deriving the related concepts and laws from other domains so that it can become an independent academic discipline. The physical education teacher must be quite conversant with the new scientific formulae that are adopted from time to time to impart up to date qualitative education. Valuable information in the form of various physical and scientific laws becomes a part and parcel of physical education. The physical educator should earnestly strive to learn the fresh knowledge and techniques so that he can teach the students and can himself be recognised as an asset of the institution, not only by the student community but also by the staff who belong to other departments and by the community at large. He should not be content with the knowledge that he should not be content with the knowledge that he has acquired from the professional institutions as well as from books and training courses. The physical educator should educator should also strive hard to evolve his own methods to realise the aims and objectives of our field. In reality society expects more from the physical educators than what is being rendered by them. This calls for greater interest, dedicated service and genuine commitments on the part on the physical educators. The educational set up in the schools and colleges will yield the desired result only if general education and physical education make a whole hearted coordinated effort in implementing the programmes successfully. General education cannot alone accomplish the onerous task of effectively educating the younger ones. There is no doubt that physical educating the younger ones. There is no doubt that physical education is part and parcel of the mainstream of general education. Physical educators stress more on active participation and not on winning or losing.

The manner in which the participants take part in competitions is more commended and appreciated. This applies to any profession. But qualitative work is admired and recognized in any walk of life rather than more quantity and volume of work personal gain is not the criterion but service to the common man and profession is all the more important. Idealistic principles will make the physical educators more dedicated towards developing the character of students. The pleasure and satisfaction that we derive from hard work, dedicated service and professional commitments are definitely unique and unparalleled. A committed individual considers his profession a field where he has to put in wholehearted effort and genuinely attempt to explore new avenues of advancement. It is a thrilling experience for a dedicated physical educator to engage himself in the development of the profession.

No doubt, the job satisfaction is personal and subjective. The professional curriculum must be planned in such a way that the trainees are given ample opportunities to educate themselves.

General Education and Physical Education

The progress of life and physical education are inseparable. Physical education is an integral part of general education as well as that of our life. In view of the vital role that it plays in our very life, we should have recognised it and adopted it effectively in general education.

It is high time that we give it the right status. There cannot be good results in the limited time allotted to the physical education classes. The time must be sufficiently increased for the efficient and effective learning of the higher values of physical education. It should get the academic status of a full-fledged branch of knowledge which will pave the way for a renaissance in all spheres of general education

The leaders of physical education blessed with foresight are striving hard to achieve this ideal. The ideal changes and reformative amendments in the principles of physical education should be carried out after deep thought and analytical scrutiny, taking into consideration three vital aspects, namely, the scope of physical education as a full-fledged academic discipline, professional ethics and the relationship with other domains.

Physical education has a relationship and correlation with different academic fields. It has to draw various physical, bio-chemical and mechanical laws from other disciplines for its enrichment. Thus the content of this field is abundantly rich. Professional ethics should take a new dimensional approach and physical education can no more be an island away from the mainstream of education. The chief aim is the all round development and fuller growth of children. Physical education cannot survive unless it receives unstained cooperation and generous help from other disciplines. The affinity and relationship between general education and physical education have fallen into oblivion in the practical sense.

Thus both exist physically together but are functionally apart. Both must go hand in hand in order to produce the desired results in the personality development of children at all levels. The physical educators should be conscious of the importance to be given to the educational perspective in physical activity. Opportunities should be open to all the pupils in educational institutions for fuller growth and prosperity. It is important that carefully chosen and meticulously planned physical activities should be included in the curriculum to enhance the active participation of the children for this development of their personality traits. It is important to evaluate the contribution of general education to the development of the culture, attitude and behavior of the people of this country. Heave we succeeded in this great task? We have made considerable improvement in the physical education programmes which have really played an important role in discriminating knowledge liberating the mind and improving skills, promoting free thinking and encouraging creative talents and developing positive attitudes towards change and order.

Society is expecting a lot from general education. A player should be analysed and judged from several angles. The physical educator should scout the all round performance of a player not only in the sportsmanly but also in the classroom and elsewhere.

The player's behavioral patterns must be scrutinised for further psychological stabilisation. There should be an ideal relationship between the classroom teachers and physical educators so that both can arrive at an analytical conclusion about the abilities, interest, limitations and scope of each individual student and his participation in the school activities. This system of studying the students helps the physical educator to assess the motor skills of the individual before the individual is permitted to practise in the specialised area. The physical educator establishes a close relationship with the teachers of other disciplines regarding nutrition, health, diseases, safety measures, first, aid, etc.

The physical educator has to cover the topics like physiology, physics, sports, medicine, first aid and he is also involved in mathematical concepts like duration of time counting measurements, sequences, evaluation, etc. Further, he has to evolve social concepts that may be developed during healthy athletic competitions and games. He should ask the students to give their views and comments after the game is over. In this way, physical education is a part of general education.

Physical education is passing through a difficult period because the State and policy makers do not come forward enthusiastically to make it an essential part of general education. The time allotted for students at lower levels as well as higher levels is not sufficient at all. Naturally, the students cannot benefit much from physical education in most schools and colleges. If at all students spend their evenings on the games field, it may be the "chosen group" participating in the school games, interclass matches and inter school tournaments which are purely carried on a voluntary basis.

The pity is that the fruits of physical education do not reach all the students. Moreover, there is no uniform pattern in the schools regarding the effective thrust on physical education with the result that it is not given the due place and importance and has thus become a matter of convenience. Generally, the teachers of general education as well as of physical education feet that general education and physical education are distinct and separate entities and do not have common educational elements.

This is the cause for several serious misconceptions among the educated masses as well as the public. They fail to recognise the interrelationship and interdependence without which the very purpose of general education is defeated. It is very interesting to note that both the subject teacher and the physical educator deal with the same material, namely the student.

The unity of organism, and the interaction between the parts are confirmed in research findings. The integration of youth personalities in educational institutions is safeguarded and promoted to the optimum level only if the forces of these twin. Related fields act on the student community. It is a fact that the examination system and thc present pattern of education contribute in making the student panic-stricken, perturbed and crippled as regards the spontaneous development of personality traits. General education cannot afford to forego the unique services of the physical educator.

He is an asset not only to the educational institutions but also to the students because his chief work is to promote their physical health as well as their intellects, emotions, sociable character, cognitive and recreational abilities.

The days are not far off when physical education will identify itself with general education. At present, this ideal identification is mostly at a verbal level. Though it is popularly said that physical education is an integral part of general education, yet it is so only theoretically.

It is however very gratifying to know that a favorable climate is now gradually being created to establish a close rapport. It is necessary that physical education should have devised a clear-cut basic concept which is conducive for such renovative outcome and mutual enrichment. This healthy relationship between general subjects and physical education should blossom in the day-to-day routine of schools and colleges which will contribute to the balanced growth psychological stability and positive outlook of the young students. The terms physical education makes us understand the educational perspective as well as physical values.

But in practice, unfortunately, we are prone to missing the educational values that are derived from physical education. In this way we miss the right perspective. The foundations of physical education and the preconditions of a proper educational perspective have not been efficiently planned and effectively executed. This deficient condition has led to academic chaos and confusion in its implementation, as a result of which a corrective formula is to be sought to put physical education on the right track. It is obvious that physical education has a great role to play in order to achieve the goals of education. But the physical educators are not aware of the potentialities it possesses. The correct approach, practical manipulations and organisational devices are not to be carried out in every educational institution by the individual physical educator alone. Both physical education and general education are inseparable and the existence and execution of one is not only unhealthy but also creates undesirable tendencies among the children. Physical education should always produce an educational value which is superb and ideal in every respect. The necessary prerequisites should be made available for the successful implementation of physical education. Here educational perspective is a precondition. There is no guarantee that we may succeed to a great extent just because of the existence of the educational perspective.

Moreover, there are other factors which determine the possibility of the correct educational perspective.

They are

a) The ample scope for interaction between groups and individuals.

b) certain physiological and biological endowments,

c) the educational institution and its multifarious on going activities.

These three factors can make a correlation between physical education and education for the purpose of transfer of learning from one to another which may not always be simple in practical situations. The educational values that the children learn from physical activities are different depending upon the teachers, coaches, facilities, playmates and available equipments. The type of educational experience acquired differs from one game to the other according to the nature movement pattern, equipment and ground as different technical and biomechanical principles are involved in them.

The scoring procedures, strategy and technical personnel very according to the game. Thus the students engaged in different physical activities receive several kinds of educational values. A gifted and brilliant student may excel both in academic performance as well as in the spheres of games and sports. It is a golden opportunity for the students to have the playing field as the educating unit where they are exposed to educative phenomena such as trial-and error learning, goals and achievements levels, appreciation and punishment, psychological stability and sportsmanship qualities. If physical activities are efficiently organised, they may positively improve the physical standards of students. Physical education programmes, like competitions between the various groups in and out of the educational institutions really help to enrich their psychological aspects. In schools and colleges, a meritorious sports performance is given due importance in matters of admission and promotions. Physical education promotes educational perspectives as it produces direct impact on the teaching learning process, organisational and administrative aspects.

This inductive function of physical education is possible only if the activities are properly planned and strictly implemented. It is not possible to give a clear cut definition of the term education. It may mean more than an ocean. It is incorrect to say that education takes place inside physical buildings or only in a limited area. It may occur in any place. The educational institutions provide opportunities for the students to spend a major portion of their time and learn the programmed and framed knowledge. In everybody's case, the institutionalised education has great impact on the formation of personality. The motto, systems and customs followed in a particular institution are reflected in the attitude and behavior of a student's life. Though physical education is an integral part of general education, it also, to a great extents supports and supplements the aims and objectives of general education.

It is a heavenly biassing that the coordinated work of general education and physical education do not contradict each other at any juncture, thus there is a greater possibility of realising the aims of education in general through the various designed programmes of physical education. Thus, it goes without saying that every physical educator should be well-versed with the precepts of general education.

Physical education should not be restricted to training in sports and games. It should play a wider role in overall education of society. It is high time that the essential values and idealistic principles of various domains of learning should be brought into the mainstream of physical education to frame an integrated programme of schooling to achieve complete and comprehensive values in the educational setup. But general education and physical education have a common task, i.e., to promote the all round development of the child, in their respective ways.

The product to be shaped and moulded is the child. The physical educator should possess necessary pre-requisites for interpreting the psychological, social and physical aspects of the total structure of schooling so that physical activities can be selected on the basis of the need, interest and abilities of the individual students and the educational objectives of the school. The educational basis of physical education should define the scope of physical education as well as form the proper guidelines to match the student with the activities relevant to schooling. Physical education, which is indeed a dynamic field, cannot afford to function in isolation in schools and colleges without associating itself with other connected disciplines.

The field of physical education involves not only students at various levels but also several personnel like the participants, parents, audience, administrators, and physical educators. So physical education is unique in this aspect because it establishes the interaction and also the interpersonal relationship between many personalities through physical activities, thus playing a predominant role in the total educational process. The physical educator must possess positive insight into his profession and have thorough knowledge about physical education as an educational process.

It makes him view the player from an educational point of view. The player who faces victory or defeat well who walks out of the field in protest the physically disadvantaged, the student who withdraws from the field the school champion, his playmates and his opponents, his captain, his coach, his officials and audience are all part of the play. So it is better that the physical educator masters the educational forces and the influences of the educational atmosphere on the player's performance and on his own coaching or training. The competitions conducted on the field should inculcate the spirit of sportsmanship and healthy competition.

The constructive competitions are designed to produce among the players educative values. The higher values emerge through the interaction of individual participants in the sports and games. Thus strong character is and exemplary personalities are evolved on the play-field. The behavioral methods and social sciences have lone been of importance and interest to those concerned with sports and physical education. Great emphasis has been laid on the intensification of academic study in physical education with respect to educational objectives and their interpretation which has resulted exciting experience Novel ideas, meanings, concepts and workable suggestions are evolved for physical educator in the classroom and the coach in the playground.

The physical educator should be prepared to accept

and babbitt to these innovative ideas. The play-field is an open-air classroom where the children go with their unique ways of life, abilities and limitations and acquire emotional stability, trial-aid-error learning and character formation. The physical educator creates through various physical activities, an educative climate from which the children learn a lot for life along, with health habits and recreative values. A physical educator should therefore have knowledge of both physical and general education.

Philosophy

The most important professional hurdle that we find in the world of today is that interested and dedicated individuals do not join the field of physical education. The physical educators are therefore largely misfits who may not be competent enough to deliver the goods. Physical education is the last resort for incompetent individuals who have no aptitude for the profession. Some individuals knowingly take temporary shelter under its fold. This sorry state of affairs generates wavering minds and indifference on the part of these. The professionals can always contribute something positively to the profession and not the wayward individuals. This type of superficial expansion is temporary and detrimental to the health and improvement of the profession. The precondition for any professional growth is thus the number of committed professionals who can discharge their professional responsibilities diligently and willingly. An individual can switch over to another profession but an intentional stay in a profession as a pastime may considerably ruin the growth of the profession and its very existence. In these days, physical educators work mainly for monetary benefits.

If not all, most of them do not have or develop the requisite enthusiasm, sincerity and dedication. If we trace the development of any profession, we find that it is because many dedicated souls have worked relentlessly. It is, no doubt, a challenging and tough task for those who wish to make physical education an independent academic discipline in this vast nation. Such sagacious leaders may have to face troubles and initial impediments, but they can gradually achieve their goal provided they have strong will to face the hurdles in their path.

Professionalism and Professional Ethics

Physical education aims at the around development of human beings, i.e., young children and adults. In the field of physical education higher virtues and sacred and sublime qualities are instilled in the minds of the students.

Physical educators play a predominant role in this aspect. They rank next to the parents in imparting decency and decorum to young ones. So the physical educator should understand that his profession needs a specific type of professional behavioral. An individual can afford to lose both wealth and health, but certainly not his character. So also an individual profession cannot afford to lose its character, namely professional image which emerges from the plans and behavior of the profession as well as the professionals.

The community at large must certify the worth and condition of any profession and not the personnel within the profession itself. The combined and coordinated efforts of all the persons at all levels can build up a positive professional image.

A single man, can by no means, succeed in this great task. Honesty and integrity of the physical educators will do a lot in this regard. The professional image is nothing but the general view that people have about a profession. Inherently, it is a psychological impression after constant and careful scrutiny of the profession. If a particular individual does not observe the code of professional ethics faithfully, he not only harms his own personal image but also ruins the already established image of the profession. Professionalisation opens up a good number of opportunities and advantageous vistas for the physical education teacher to pedogenic and face new problems connected with his subject in an appropriate manner. The physical educators are trained in such a way that they are well-equipped professionally to adjust ant adapt to the new changes and professional regulations that are introduced from time to time.

It is evident that the regulations can participate in a healthy manner in the interdisciplinary approaches and intellectual discussions with the teachers of other academic disciplines. At present, this intellectual interaction is not very much in practice, because of the language problem or the limited acquaintance with other disciplines.

Hence to further our own interest of getting accepted by other professionals from other disciplines, we should be professionalised in our discipline and be recognised with due honor as fellow teachers in the totality of the entire educational system.

It is clearly understood now that professional ethics include

a) a code of conduct,

b) the philosophy of the profession,

c) a dignity of work,

d) a professional attitude,

e) a commitment and

f) job satisfaction

Professional ethics can be called a psychological state of mind derived out of a voluntary exposure to a profession. Hasty action, likes and dislikes, personal attachments, sentimental influences and biased opinions have no place in a profession and an individual must take up his profession as a noble one and give it his due regard and respect. A true and ideal professional always seeks to do something in his cherished field as his contribution and this professional thirst does not end till he creates a suitable environment for the betterment of the existing conditions of the profession.

A committed physical educator is an asset to his discipline and he can be entrusted with confidential responsibilities and professional commitments because he will be prepared to make all-out attempts for utilising his potentialities and talents for the betterment of him profession. The achievements in any academic discipline is due to such committed individuals. It is quite obvious that a trained professional in any branch of knowledge, especially in physical education, is bound to develop and possess his or her own attitude about the profession he has embraced for either livelihood or service.

The physical educator should avoid forming subjective attitudes. The individual must analyse the overall situation and the impact of it before forming final attitudes, judgement and decisions. This can be achieved only when an individual is able to estimate the real situations, and infer or inter pert them with an open mind and welcome these situations irrespective of his personal likes and dislikes. Professional ethics includes the practical attitudes of the person towards his profession and the estimation and value that he attaches to it. The healthy attitudes about the profession to which an individual is wedded must duly generate the right type of spirit, drive which ultimately leads to the desired target.

Physical education involves group competition, the social gathering and togetherness of a host of individuals who try hard for individual as well as common goals wherein we find mixed causes and effects such as competition and cooperation, winning and losing, risk and safety. The element of risk involved in the field of physical education right from the training phase till the actual competition is to be borne in mind by the different personnel involved in physical education and sports namely of coaches, managers and sportsmen. The ethical aspects of a profession should be flexible, functional and operational so as to be conducive to conducive to attaining higher and holistic virtues and values.

A rigid set of professional ethics may not produce the desired results. Moreover, the tremendous toil and dedicated service rendered by many become futile and fruitless. The physical educators must, as far as possible, try to follow these ethics. It is necessary to provide better working conditions and privileges to the physical educators so as to motivate them. T'.e distribution of duties and responsibilities amongst various segments of the community makes thew administrative machinery strong and smooth.

The real strength of any profession lies not only in its productivity but perhaps, more so, in its ethical behavioral. Productivity is discernible whereas the effect of ethical behavior assumes long-term significance. Physical education can in no way boast of having the professional ethics that every other profession has been fortunate enough to possess.

To cite an example, professions like medicine and law have well laid out codes of professional ethics which enhance their morale and promote their image. As these two professions have unique roles to play in the modern world, numerous other professions too have got a predominant part to play. Physical education ethics do inspire the physical education to participate in the professional programmes and variety of commitments in wholesome ways in order to achieve the aims and objectives of physical education. When the physical educator fail to follow the professional ethics., they are bound to create problems of great magnitude.

They may not understand the disadvantages and serious ill-effects that arise on account of the breach of the professional ethics in the beginning but in the long run it leads to the disorganisation of their own personality because of the continuous development of themselves complex and finally their behaviour cannot be justified either by themselves or by observers.

It is no exaggeration to say that the absence of professional ethics causes inconsistent attitude and behaviour patterns among the physical educators. This sorry state of affairs in the field of physical education breeds conflicts, chaos, unwanted comments from others and an unpleasant atmosphere at the end. It is crystal clear that physical educators should strictly follow the ethical values and virtues. Professional ethics denotes professional standards and norms of conduct for people who have dedicated themselves to serve the community at large through these coordinated programmes.

The rules and regulations that are framed in any profession serve like a guiding star to the people who are directly or indirectly involved. The ethical formulae maintain the moral standard of the general social attitude and way of life. The professionals have no personal ambition to achieve. In this process of dedicated service, the physical educators have to sacrifice their personal benefits. Such sacrifices and dedicated involvement by the physical educators contribute a lot to the growth of the profession. The individual should be prepared to accept the great task for the sake of bringing honour and glory to the profession. The codes of a field are a strong base on which the future of the profession, as well as of the personnel, involved is dependent to a great extent. Professional ethics should be given top priority especially in the organisation and administration of professional concepts in an educational institution. It vividly points out the do's and don'ts thereby helping the physical educator to get rid of the areas of conflicts and controversy.

The physical educators are quite aware of, and conversant with the ideal ways and means of putting into practice the systematic approaches and ideal methods of the profession. The guiding principles of professional ethics are a must for specific action and accomplishment in the ever-changing routine and roles of physical educators. The physical educators should welcome and appreciate the professional codes for the betterment of their profession. It is important to note that rules and concepts are for the profession.

The professional ethics emerge within the framework of the profession itself which may be the result of the experiences acquired and the amalgamated opinions and constructive views of the co-physical educators of various correlated backgrounds. The physical educators are morally bound to observe professional ethics as there are no hard and fast rules to punish the defaulters in case they fail to follow.

But the social pressures from the professional associations, etc., are the usual social penalties for violating professional ethics. Every physical educator is expected to be more responsible to adhere to the ethics framed. Though the code of professional ethics is applicable to teachers in general, the physical educators are particularly expected to practise it sincerely so as to set a good example for others.

There are lot of opportunities in physical education programmes such as fair play, good sportsmanship, cooperation, unselfishness, regard for rules of games and fellowship, etc. The physical educators should lead a clean academic as well as social life, failing which they earn a bad name for the physical education community and the profession too.

Suggested Master Plan

1. The aims and objectives of physical education should be defined in clear-cut terms.

2. The close-knit relationship of physical education with other disciplines should be understood and established in an appropriate way so as to obtain the maximum benefits.

3. The concept and utility of movement patterns which form the basis of all types of labour and managerial affairs should be rightly appreciated.

4. Different bodies and individuals should be amalgamated to make united effort to achieve the full-fledged academic status for physical education.

5. It is of prime importance that experts and stalwarts from other fields are requested to put their heads and hearts together to make a better design for physical education by making them participate in lectures, seminars and workshops.

6. Short refresher courses may be held for physical educators to raise the standard of physical education as well as maximise their contribution to the field.

7. The various quarters should be convinced of the importance and need of physical education so that will whole heartedly patronise the steps that the physical educators undertake. The governments at the centre and states should give priority to the physical educators in the matters of employment.

Physical education is a unique field where there are

ample opportunities for demonstration of action and strict observance of rules.

It is not to be found in other disciplines. The importance of self is stressed emphatically though the ultimate goal is to inculcate the feelings of group spirit, group interaction and group welfare and service before self. This is, no doubt, a special feature of physical education. The potentialities and scope of physical Education are tremendous and they should be released, and the conceptual framework and foundation should also be rationalized to pave the way for a renaissance in physical education.

It is possible only through reformulating the theoretical perspective. Physical education grows naturally, provided it has a strong academic status which helps in freer and fuller growth. Apart from this, this status helps to bring about an intellectual harmony, understanding and cooperation between the various personalities, agencies and associations involved in this field. This naturally facilitates the evolution of a sound and practicable theory for the purpose of learning these activities effectively. Educational objectives are carefully planned in such a way as to inculcate social, moral and holistic virtues in the minds of young children, thereby making them fit personalities in this complicated and competitive world.

Education as well as physical education plays a vital role to achieve this unique ambition. No doubt, in modern life, parents cannot always afford to spare sufficient attention towards educating the young ones. The teachers are also not in a position to do justice as there is limited time at their disposal. Even if the teachers are prepared to render dedicate their selfless service to educate the students in a special and better manner, the students are not only unreceptive but they look down upon both the physical education teachers and the entire programme as it does not enjoy a reputation like other subjects.

Students also do not consider physical education as part of general education. These programmes are distinctly and decidedly alienated from the mainstream of education as they have been eternally branded, in practice, as the optional and extra evening hour programmes which have no value and significance in the academic, social and professional spheres. Physical education has unfortunately lost its significance as it is not a subject for examination and gradation in the strictest sense. Invariable, the students, the society and even the teaching community give it stepmothers treatment and less importance in curriculums at all levels. Everybody is privileged and entitled to choose his or her or her own branch of knowledge and pursue for personal and social betterment. Educational institutions which have the moral and legal duty to cater to the genuine needs of the growing students according to their capacity and capability and resources and aspirations neither provide adequate facilities, amenities, and resources and aspirations neither provide adequate facilities, amenities, and congenial atmosphere for young ones to take up a sporting career, nor regularise the time meant for physical education programmes. In this aspect, we have utterly disappointed the students of our days and they have been deprived of the privilege of enjoying the benefits of physical education. The result is that they do not flock with enthusiasm to the fields nor do they stick to physical education activities for a long time.

Philosophy and Physical Education

In variably all the branches of knowledge emerge from philosophy which vividly indicates the vital role that philosophy plays at every phase in all walks of life. We cannot separate or segregate philosophy from any discipline. Physical education has or has to have the essential elements and tenets of philosophy, as it has a predominant part in the development of the total personality of a child. General education does have the relevant maximum relationship with philosophy.

Philosophical analysis and values have contributed considerably to the formation of educational practices. Motivation plays a vital part in encouraging the students, trainees and the physical educators themselves to gain inspiration and intellectual information and must work towards providing an independent status to the subject but not at the cost of discarding the role of philosophy in physical education. In today's changing society, there must be a sound philosophy of physical education for the profession to survive and flourish. Philosophy is a process through which physical educators search for truths, reality and values. It is only through philosophy that physical educators are able to study the meaning, nature, importance and source of values in physical education.

Philosophy guides the physical educator in determining the aims, objectives, principles and content of physical education and provides a logical means of determining whether or not it is providing worth while services in the education of human beings. A professional philosophy has the superb inherent ability to inspire the professional to act with vigor and vitality, conviction and contemplation to the fullest possible cxtent. The essential elements of philosophy are eventually reflected in his mind, words and deed. The mind, local system and psychomotor system generate positive thinking, positive speaking and positive speaking and positive doing. The congenial blend of these three vital aspects goes astray if the individual does not strictly follow the professional ethics and philosophical values in actual practice.

It is of the utmost importance that the training systems include both the professional ethics as well as the philosophy along with other departments of knowledge in the professional institutions. Otherwise, the training is an incomplete one which produces imbalances and inconsistencies among the physical educators. Ever since the recorded history, philosophy has solid and strong foundations for almost all domains of knowledge.

Physical education is no exception. Educational thought is influenced by the five major philosophies, viz., idealism, realism, pragmatism, naturalism and existentialism. A physical educator must have the basic knowledge of the concept of philosophy that can be practised in everyday life. Any physical educator must have the basic knowledge of the concept of philosophy that can be practised in everyday life. Any physical educator who has mastered or has been blessed inherently with this gift can succcssfully do a better job in the institutions and can better match the students and sports appropriately, instead of falling into the trap of mechanical and routine working. The physical educator should strive to inculcate in the young minds of the students a well-balanced philosophical outlook vis-a-vis the overall sports programmes. The field and concept of physical education do not enjoy any remarkable reputation and important status as most people are not convinced of the importance of physical education in day-to-day life. There have been many great men in every field who were not physically strong. So, there is a school of thought that the physical weakness may not be a hindrance or hurdle to achieving greatness or name.

It is not correct to say that physically weak people develop other compensatory capacities either to be on par with the normal ones or to excel them in every aspect. Most people are not conscious of the necessity of living a wholesome and healthy life. In ordinary life, men like to reach the pinnacle of greatness by hook or by crook. The vital pint of healthy living is ignored or totally discarded.

But the very same people whole heartedly precise the physical fitness assignments. It is of interest to trace the historical development of physical education. Many scientists, philosophers and psychologists have propounded theories of physical education in depth and breadth in the light of scientific principles. Aristotle made an extensive study of the systems of the human body and its practical functions in relation to physical activities.

Physical education vividly depicts the ever growing social changes and the changes causes in the structure and implementation of objectives of education. Its nature and content open new avenues for experimentation and exploration in the field which will pave the way for its total development. It cannot be accorded the status of an academic discipline as it does not satisfy the prerequisites at present.

But physical educators are striving ceaselessly to establish its worth. Though we may succeed in making physical Education a full-fledged academic discipline, it will not function as an independent discipline unless there is a drastic move on the part of the government to promote it. Physical eductors have arrived at the conclusion, after serious discussions and analysis, that physical activities have definite correlation and interrelationship with other branches of knowledge. This has led to the promotion of the nature, purpose, status and scope of physical education. The leaders of physical education have done their best to explore the influences of various social, physical, cultural and psychological phenomena upon physical activities. This is not sufficient. A strong nationwide educational policy is required to amalgamate the various factors to bring about sequential coherence among the various faculties which can stir up human activity and the acquisition of skills. We cannot but admit the fact that vital concepts such as motivational methods, aspiration levels and self-evaluation have not attained significance and due place in practice. The concept of physical education and its programmes at various levels have to be restructured and modified according to the present conditions and needs so as to enable the modern child to enjoy the fullest possible benefits of physical education.

Then only can it become a meaningful part of general education. The present move is to establish physical education as a compact and complete academic subject which can magnificently kindle the spark and bring out the hidden talents and aspirations in a consecutive constructive manner. At present, physical educators have resolved to change the age-old concept of physical education as it was considered to be the one hour evening programme. In other words, it is nothing but one period physical exercises or events.

In other words, it is nothing but one period physical exercises or events. In reality, it is not so. It has got a tremendous role to play at school, college and university levels. The potentialities and idealistic virtues of men should be spotted out and exploited to the maximum or else the aims and objectives of education and physical education are totally defeated. Moreover, the physical educators should not be content with their professional services in the educational institutions, if they fail to contribute to the actual development of personalities at their disposal. It is a period of transition for both education and physical education.

They have to cope with the new changes and satisfy the pressing demands. They should unhesitating adopt newly discovered ways and means in their approaches to shape the personality of a growing child. Then they can deliver the goods in a fitting manner. Today the world is highly competitive in nature.

Physical education is no exception. It goes without saying that the programmes of physical education should be restyled and tailored to suit the present conditions in the educational institution. Unless every facet of academic discipline is given the right place, education cannot but be a dismal failure. Physical education promotes the whole being of man namely the body mind and spirit to suitable and necessary highest level. So, it is to make physical education an academic discipline. Invariable all the physical educators are giving a clarion call for standardising the academic status of physical education. They try all out means to make it a full-fledged academic discipline. Unfortunately various efforts like well intended seminars, etc., have not helped in getting physical education a respectable status in educational institution. It has been deprived of its legitimate, rignt and was made to have a secluded existence for name's sake, which did not create high esteem among physical educators themselves. Conversely, they were more likely to develop an inferiority complex. The physical educators were openly branded and treated as second rate persons compared to the classroom teachers. The prime work to be undertaken is to make them feel strongly that physical education is on par with other branches and faculties of knowledge.

They should have the necessary conviction on this point. Unless physical education marches majestically along with other disciplines, the realisation of the goals of education in the true sense is impossible. A dynamic master plan should be evolved to re arrange the course of action for making physical education an effective medium to achieve the desired ends of general education. The following suggestions may bring about good results.

11

RESEARCH METHODOLOGY IN PHYSICAL EDUCATION

The descriptive method of research deals with the sciences, physical or social, and performs certain essential functions such as description, explanation, prediction and control. It has to about various methods for releasing these functions. The descriptive method is one such used by scientists, particularly the social scientists. The descriptive method is the simplest one and is applicable to a number of social problems.

It is essentially a fact-finding approach related largely to the present and abstracting generalisations arrived at by a cross-sectional study of the current situation. It comprised mainly collection of data; but mere collection is not research. So, the descriptive method to some extent also interprets the data. The social scientist sees to it that his research finding is arrived at after following methodical processes and procedures like observation, explanation, interpretation and generalisation of the data gathered. As a matter of fact there are multi-facetious problems in society and the social problems which crop up then and there lend themselves to the descriptive study.

The problems in the social fields are larger in

number than can be studied through the application of this method. The types of problems covered here include describing the characteristics of communities, establishing the proportion of people in a specified population who hold certain views or attitudes or who behave in certain ways, and discovering of testing whether certain variables are associated. Some specific trend or prediction studied may also fall under this category: whether the popularity of a sportsman is declining over a period of time or how many people will attend a national level football match. Writers have different opinions on how to classify the descriptive studies.

The broad classification of the descriptive method is as follows; survey analysis; school surveys; job analysis; documentary analysis; community surveys. There is no hard and feast rule that the descriptive method has to be limited to any one method of data collection.

There are no bounds or any restriction on the employment of methods. They may make use of any or all of the methods like observation, questionnaire, interviewing and scaling techniques used by social scientist. Although descriptive studies may be a wide range of techniques, this does not mean that they are characterised by the flexibility that marks exploratory studies.

The procedure to be used in a descriptive study must be carefully planned. Because the aim is to obtain complete and accurate information, the design must make much more provision for protection against bias than required in exploratory studies. Because the amount of work involved in descriptive studies frequently concerns economy of research, this effort is extremely necessary and significant. The major steps such as formulating the objectives of the study, designing the methods of data collection, selecting the sample, collecting and checking the data and analyzing the results are the main steps in a descriptive investigation. The investigator must take utmost care of the limitations that are found in this method.

The researcher may make description an end in itself as the research is essentially creative and demands the discovery of facts in order to lead to a solution of the problem. As problems in social sciences are of a continue nature, the researchers should have a progressive outlook in finding solutions to them, otherwise it leads to complacency and conservatism. A second limitation lies in going to the other extreme where the statistical technique dominates. The desire to overemphasis central tendencies and to present the facts in terms of averages, correlation co-efficients, means, and dispersions may not always be either necessary or welcome.

This limitation arises because statistics, which is partly a descriptive tool of analysis, can help, but not always explain, the casual relations or correlations between variables.

Historical Research

In common parlance, we come across people jokingly saying, "history is a mystery." But in reality, it cannot be considered so because history tells about the very concrete past or actual happenings in the past with a bit of exaggeration as the historians have the legitimate licence to make their narration colorful and inspiring. It will of course, be futile to expect only facts as the narration is affected by the writer's bias and prejudices. Historically, research in our civilisation has been profoundly influenced by early discoveries.

The discovery of fire, the wheel, numbers and the alphabet, paper and the process of printing; the development of metals and agriculture; and the use of steam and electricity have all been milestones in the development and refinement of civilisation. More recently have come the use of atomic power and the penetration of outer space, which in a very real sense are the culmination of long years of research and development.

History

History is a meaningful record of human achievements. It is not merely a list of chronological events but a truthful, integrated account of the relationship between persons, events, time and places. We use history to understand the past, and to understand the present in the light of past events and developments. Historical analysis may be directed toward an individual, an idea, a movement, or an institution. However, none of these objects of historical observation can be considered in isolation.

People cannot be subjected to historical investigation without some consideration of their interaction with the ideas, movements or institutions of their times. The focus merely determines the points of emphasis toward which historians direct their attention. "Historia" is a Greek term from which the term "history" has been derived and history can be rightly called the present mirror for the past events, achievements, political or social changes, etc. It reflects the wholesome picture of the life of the men who lived in yester-years. In early days, human history included a study of the past problem.

The main task of historians was to collect information about the past events and to analyse them correctly. History or historical books, therefore, mainly dealt with the life and deeds of important persons. In history books, record of kings or their army commanders and great men are also found, with a view to interpreting past events. A new method of research, known as the "historical method" came into being.

In the social sciences the historical method is used as an aid to visualising society as a bionomic organism. Human society is an terminally dynamic structure.

History is a record of changing processes. This is why, in social sciences, a study of the social processes is so revealing and important. According to Hans Garth, Every model of social structure implies a model of socio-historical change; history consists of changes which social structures undergo.

In the historical study of a social structure, the casual relation between the various aspects becomes known. The current structure, culture, folkways and social moves and organisation of any social group are resultants of its past forces, that is, its history and evolution. The knowledge about these processes enables us to anticipate their future structure.

No social change takes place in void; it is a result of

past forces and will give rise to future forces. Accordingly, in order to understand effectively any social group or institution, it has to be studied in its perspective. History enlarges the range of observed phenomena, affords a sense of mutuality of institutions and suggests conditioning factors in contemporary life. In this way, the social scientist studies the past to gain a better understanding of the present state of affairs. Though the contemporary ethyls and culture of any society is quite different from its past character, yet the seeds of the present are in the past and the contemporary modes and mores of a society are nothing but an evolution of the forces working in the past. When a research is conducted on the basis of historical data, the researcher is said to have followed the historical approach. At times, it would appear that all research is historical in its nature because, to a very large extent, research depends upon observations which are non-repetitive. Historical facts cannot be repeated in an accurate fashion as can be done in laboratory observations. Historical research involves very intensive very intensive use of library material and requires patience on the part of the researcher to deliver into the historical records.

It is essential that the problem treated with this approach is historical in nature. Only such problems as are based on historical records can be investigated by following this approach. The historical approach to research, may or may not be formulated depending upon the nature of investigation. In historical records, an attempt is usually made to establish the hypothesis formulated by a researcher. The interpretation of research data entirely depends upon the researcher himself and shall depend upon how objectively he carries out his job of interpreting the historical evidence. Therefore, it is very hard to disprove a hypothesis of the researcher and on the other hand he may conveniently make data bear upon his conclusions. Historians, philosophers, social phytochemists, literary men, as well as social scientists, use historical approach as an aid in visualising society as a dynamic organism and its structures and functions as steadily growing and undergoing change and transformation. The following words of George Bernard Shaw hold good for all time. The past is not behind the group; it is within the group. The past, if it can be located, contains the key to the present. Though today is different from yesterday, today and yesterday will probably influence tomorrow. As the famous historian, rather Schlesinger says, no individual, let alone a social scientist, can wisely ignore the long arm of the past.

One should not push the problems of time into the background. Direct observation of social phenomena in a state of rest is not sufficient foundation for study. There must be added a study of the development of these phenomena in time, that is, in history. Young has said. The historical method is the induction of the members, through resent. Dosaze has rightly said, "To be significant, social history must be a study of the various forces that bring it about" History can be functional inasmuch as humanity can profit by past experiences in the solution of present-day problems.

Sources of Historical Data

Historical research should be encouraged because it is related to the heritage of the field. No established profession has depth, traditions, customs, or a present without a history. This heritage should be recorded and preserved for future generations. The origin, growth, and development of the field; the problems faced and solved; the cultural forces exerted, the movements that have waned and persisted; the changes in implements, facilities, and costumes; the thoughts and deeds of the pioneers and leaders who shaped the profession over the years; and many other factors are subjects for historical research.

We may generally confine ourselves to three major sources of historical information:

i) documents and various historical sources to which the historian has access;

ii) materials of cultural history and of analytical history; and

iii) personal sources i.e. authentic observers and witness.

When, how and under what circumstances, to use any or all of these sources depends a great deal upon the description of the student his interests, the scope of his study and the availability of these sources. Many of the sources indispensable for adequate knowledge of the past include diaries, memoirs, concessions, autobiographies, secret archives, diplomatic agreements, uncoordinated statistical material, under-cover trade agreements, cold-straggled invention and countless other data. The related literature provides the main source of information in historical research.

The documents serve as the reports of events

consisting of impressions made on some human brain by past events and consciously or deliberately recorded for the purpose of transmitting information. The evaluation of documents is of crucial importance to enable the researcher to place each bit of information in its proper perspective and draw sound conclusions. The evaluation of historical evidence is usually known as historical criticism, which is generally divided into two groups, namely,

1) external criticism or Henristics which means inciting to find out or guiding in discovery, and

2) internal criticism or hermeneutics or interpretative criticism. The Main aim of these two types of criticism is to pronounce whether a given idea is acceptable as a fact or not. Events, occurrences and happenings as presented in the records may or may not conform to reality, for they might have been distorted twisted or misinterpreted. Thus, through these methods the authenticity and credibility of the data is tested.

External criticism is concerned with the genuineness of the document, i.e., testing the authenticity and credibility of the data. In other words external criticism deals with data relating to form and appearance rather than meaning or contents.

External criticism is sometimes called lower criticism because it is a preliminary preparatory step providing the data to be used in the second phase known as internal criticism. In testing the genuineness of a document the problem of external criticism involves the question of authorship and his qualifications as a reporter, factors or conditions that may have influenced the production of the document, such as time, place, purpose and circumstances of compositions and the extent to which the document reads true to the original. In determining the truth and value of the document, the researcher has to go into the question of authorship, his personality, character, position, general qualifications as reporter special qualification or disqualification as a reporter of the matter, interest in the events, his technical knowledge for learning and reporting the events, the ability and technique, method of writing the document from memory, after consolation with others, the data and year of documentation and such other details. On the contrary, *internal criticism* evaluates the accuracy and value or worth of the statements within the document. In other words, it is testing the credibility of the data.

This process is also called higher criticism. A historical researcher must put his documentary evidence to the test of truthfulness as well as competence. At times, many authentic or genuine documents may not be completely accurate or truthful and require internal criticism in the form of textual critics as well as investigation of such factors as the competence, good faith position and bias of the author of the document.

Internal criticism involves a scientific examination of the relevance of the data, correction of errors, and rejection of the information that is found wanting. Internal criticism is much more difficult than external one because it involves evaluating the writer, his bias, and his possible motives for distortion. This evaluation requires wide knowledge, practical experience and a training in psychology.

There are two types of internal criticism: (i) negative criticism and (ii) positive criticism. The negative criticism examines the circumstances and surroundings in which a person wrote the document, whether he was in a position to ascertain the truth and to reveal the real story and whether he was guided by motives or bias. Positive criticism seeks to find out whether the contents of the documents are true or otherwise.

In historical research, both negative and positive criticism are essential. History has attained a certain degree of maturity as a social science.

The problem that remains is that of making more explicit as a matter of practice the status already recognised in principle, of making investigation more precise, and demonstration more vigour. This is a problem that history, in company with other sciences, has always to face.

Modern Historians

Few modern historians cling to the great-man theory of history, and a few give merely episodic or dramatic fragments of events. Most modern historians present a cross-section of a level of life and events, of similarities and common traits, of the collective life of mankind. In brief they are interested in the social process as a seamless web. They realise that a collection of historical events about politics, law, economic activities and development, religion and other aspects of life would not constitute a history of mankind. The social process as a whole must also be synthesized and explained.

Advantages of the Historical Approach

The advantages of the historical approach are, of course, numerous and, after almost things under the sun and above occur in a cyclic fashion with a bit of expected or unexpected changes because change is the only reality of the cosmos.

i) Some problems are such that they can be investigated only by this approach and may not offer themselves to other approaches. Therefore, the historical approach fills in a big gap of making the research possible and also meaningful on the problems that would otherwise have remained unexplored. Many a time it is of considerable interest to use time-series data for assessing the progress or the impact of several policies and initiatives, and this can be done by looking into historical records only. For such problems, therefore, only the historical approach would be suitable.

ii) Secondly, historical data are not repeatable under any circumstances and, therefore, the historical approach serves as a ready-to-hand method to the researcher whose problems depend on historical observations.

It is fairly easy to repeat observations in laboratories under controlled conditions but this cannot be done in case in case of historical data. The historical approach, therefore, has an advantage to offer the past data under the prevailing conditions then and affords an opportunity to the researcher to view these observations in the past setting.

iii) Thirdly, historical records provide very useful information that goes a long way towards the solution of a research problem. As already said, the researcher is compelled to fall back upon the past since he cannot create these afresh and hence it is highly advantageous to follow the historical approach where the use of time series data is unavoidable in any case.

Steps in the Historical Method

The historical method studies the problems in a broad manner. This study involves certain steps which are enumerated as follows:

1. Formulation of a thesis or a report

2. The selection of the problem

3. The collection of data

4. The historical evaluation and analysis

5. Analysis and processing of data

Precautions for Persons adopting the Historical Method

A person who adopts the historical method has to be cautions. He should safeguard against certain drawbacks and defects so that study may not be spoiled by lack of objectivity or failure of presenting historical facts in proper perspective. The precautions to be taken are enumerated below:

1. Over generalisation;

2. Over simplification;

3. Choice of conjectural

4. Failure to distinguish between important and unimportant facts;

5. Failure to interpret the terms of the past;

Adequacy of Historical Data

The historical data may be regarded as reliable and adequate only.

i) when it is presented as a complex of social forces;

ii) when social phenomena meaningfully depict intricate social processes; and

iii) when a set of interrelationships—psychological, economic, educational, political and religions–contribute to a unified whole, a configuration of complex pattern.

History can be regarded as a social science that needs little argument. Historians have long been aware of their responsibility as social scientists. They have consistently affirmed the necessity of unloosing historical data rigorously. For some generations, the practice as well as the philosophy of historians have reflected a scientific spirit; and historical studies exhibit modes of thinking directly traceable tom the methods of social scilla science.

Evaluation of Historical Materials

External Criticism

1. Who is the author?

2. Was the document written by a ghost writer or by a genuine person?

3. What were the qualifications of the author?

4. Is a particular item of equipment, piece of apparatus, costume, of other professional artifact authentic?

Internal Criticism

1. Is the meaning of the words the same?

2. Is the author writing seriously?

3. Is the author expressing his or her real beliefs?

4. How soon after the event was the document written?

5. Was the author biased in any way?

6. Are written sources evaluated with an understanding of the times and conditions under which they were produced?

Limitations

The historical approach is not free from limitations. The main drawbacks of this approach are:

i) Non-matching situations,

ii) Over-generalisation, and

iii) subjective interpretations.

i*) Non-matching Situations*

A serious shortcoming of the historical approach is that am past situation cannot be matched to an existing situation. A past situation might have been influenced by social economic and political factors which are no longer the and hence present comparability of the past to the present can easily be questioned. This is more so in social sciences where it is very difficult to keep the socii-economic conditions and other dimensions of the problems under control. These days particularly when far reaching changes are occurring in society owing to rapid advancements in science and technology as a result of which social patterns are also fast changing, such non-comparability of past historical situations becomes all the more a very serious limitation in the application of the historical approach to research.

ii) *Over-generalisations*

Secondly, it has been observed the researchers with this approach tend to overgenerous their results. This sometimes leads to implausible explanations and inaccurate specifications of the research problem. Sometimes also, the results may be generalised beyond reasonable limits and these may lead to misunderstanding of historical process.

iii) *Subjective Interpretation*

Thirdly, there are great possibilities of a researcher adopting a subjective interpretation in order to validate his hypothesis. The loss of objectivity in such cases can lead to considerable inaccuracies in research findings. In social sciences, the scope for subjective interpretation is large because socio-economic variables are complex in nature and can be interpreted in different ways. In spite of the honest efforts of a researcher circumstances may compel him to go in for subjective in trepidations at the cost of objective analysis only to defend his findings which could otherwise be challenged or disproved by other researchers. Subjectivity of interpretations is, therefore, a basic limitation of the historical approach to research.

Limitations may also arise in the writing of history itself because

i) Not all happenings in time and space can be known at the time of writing, and

ii) Historians cannot write history life-size

iii) personal bias and private interpretations often enter unconsciously, even when honest attempts are made to elect pertinent facts, to arrange them consistently, and to place them in a coherent and true frame of reference.

However, it should be observed that this approach cannot be dispensed with as a large number of problems cannot be investigated in the absence of historical research. Many a time, it would be desirable for researchers to look into historical records to have better insight into their own investigation.

It is quite obvious that history repeats itself with the same reflection and proportion in our own time. The behavioral pattern does not depend upon the past or the future but on the present. Modern historians are interested in the cultural changes. There always exists a connecting link between experiences and present attitudes and values. Moreover, the historical events are closely interwoven with the social life of men.

It is natural that a novice doing historical research may ask: "Why should a man concern himself with old records compiled and written long ago by persons of varied interests and points of view"? There can be no two opinions that these traces of past events stored away in dry documents contribute to an understanding of life, generations or centuries later. The question of whether or not the historical method is scientific has often been debated.

Generally, early historians wrote history more as an instrument of propaganda; their purpose was to glorify the cause espoused, whether it be the state, the church, a given organisation or institution, or the perpetuation of the memory of a public servant or professional pioneer. Certainly the historical method so employed was far from scientific. Before the nineteenth century, history as a science was generally unknown. The contention is made, however, that modern historians exhibit scientific characteristics in that critically and objectively investigate their source materials; they formulate and evaluate hypotheses; they make explanations, tentatively at least of the occurrence of events or conditions.

But unlike scientists, historians cannot test their hypotheses by direct experimentation; they cannot employ controlled observation. Original conditions cannot be repeated; history cannot be re-enacted. The primary function of science is to get at the true facts, or probabilities, as precisely as possible, by weighing all the available evidence. Historical evidence can be evaluated. Cause-and-effect relationships and the predictions of outcomes, after the manner of other sciences, however, are not so readily realised by historical method. Actually, the scholar of physical education need not be unduly concerned as to whether the historical method is or is not scientific.

It is sufficient to know that certain sources of evidence are available for historical study, that these sources can be appropriately evaluated, that generalisations regarding the past can be made and that hypotheses relative to the future can be proposed. The method of history must be understood and rigidly followed if historical studies are to be worthy of note.

Case Study

A case study is an in-depth and diagnostic study which provides perfect types of sociological material as they represent a more enlightening and fundamentally more real record of personal experiences with a wealth of concrete detail, vivid memories, tension, situation which escape the attention of most skilled investigators. Using other techniques. According to S.P. Sukha the main characteristics of a good case study are: the completeness of the data; the validity of the data; continuity; confidential recording, and scientific synthesis. The case study helps to probe the entire life-span of a social unit intensively and to analyse the entire life-span of a social unit intensively and to analyse the complex factors that influence the social unit.

It also covers a wide range of information about the cases. Thus, it gives a greater depth of knowledge and experience which may be of great use for further research. The case data are vivid, absorbing and tend to reproduce a person's social attitudes and values and facilitate the researcher to understand everything about a social unit and the variety of habits, traits and qualities within a social unit. Moreover, it effectively helps to secure detailed information about the growth of the unit, group structures, individual life pattern, etc., and its and its techniques are often used in pure research, sociology and economics with a view to develop certain theories and broad principles. The case studies are indispensable for therapeutic administrative purposes. It is also easy to generalis cases with the help of a case study and prepare a plan of action for treatment. It is also followed for comparison, classification, analysis and for the formulation of a hypothesis leading to further research.

It is highly useful for the researcher's framing of schedules, questionnaires, furnishing clues for further research, diagnosis and other case-by-case problems. Though the case study method has contributed much to social research, some social scientists have raised some objections against the value and validity of case studies.

In the practical research experimentation, social scientists have attributed some limitations to case studies. It is obvious that the case study does not provide universal impersonal and common aspects of a phenomenon. There is a tendency for a researcher to draw generalisations after studying a few cases, which may not be relevant to all situations and there is a tendency to overemphasize the unique or unusual events which are seldom comparable. The subjective data collected do not lend themselves to quantitative checks and it is costly, time-consuming and wasteful in certain cases where the objectives are limited.

It is the general view that the case study is loose and unsystematic and the generalisations drawn from a few cases are not always accurate. The basic drawback in the case study is that there is a temptation to ignore the basic principles of research design. But most of the problems can be avoided through improved techniques of case studies. Social scientists like Carl Rogers, Elton Mayo, Mirra Komarousky, and Alfred Kinsey have used the new techniques of collecting, recording and processing case data.

Thus they have made the case study as one of the important methods of social research. It is obvious that a case study is a form of research methodology and it has got different meanings in different disciplines. But still, it has definite and particular connotations in every individual branch of knowledge. For example, in medicine, it is the close examination of an ailing person or patient. In the education atmosphere, it may concern the various problems of a student or teacher or the institution. The case study may very well mean a unit of study in which the unit may be a person or episode or the life of a person, a group of persons, historical offenders, etc. The case selected may be a deviant case, a negative case, a typical case and an extreme case. While every case study is unitary, it is also complex, whole and unique and a case can be non-comparable, non-additive and non-qualitative data.

But as a matter of fact, the case study is a qualitative analysis. Like other terms, the term case too implies different disciplines and professions, depending upon the nature and status. It may mean, in medicine, an ailing person who has approached the practitioner for necessary treatment. In education the maladjusted students, other difficulties of a student and educational institutions with peculiar problems constitute a case.

In the field of sociology, it may refer to a person with an intrapsychic or inter-personal problem. Social scientists, in their study of human behaviour, strive to obtain a fundamentally real and enlightened record of personal experiences which would reveal in concrete detail man's inner striving, tension, and motivations, that drive him or challenge him, the forces that direct him to adopt a certain pattern of behaviour and to live according to a certain scheme and philosophy of life. Only some of man's experiences can be learned by observing him in action.

To understand his behaviour fully and intimately, he must supply a detailed and penetrating account of what he does and has done what he expects to do, and says he ought to do. Social scientists study many culture groups, small social groups.

They also study large groups, as social units social institutions. Case data may be gathered exhaustively, of an entire life circle of a social unit or a definite section of it.

Whether a section or the whole of a life is studied, the aim is to ascertain the natural history, that is, an account of the genetic development of a person or group or whatever constitutes the social unit in a particular study, revealing the factors that moulded the life of the unit within its cultural setting.

Because of its aid in studying behaviour in specific, precise detail, Burgess termed the case study method as "The Social Microscope". The case study is a very popular method of collecting information about the personal life of an individual, or a group of persons. This has been in vogue for so many years.

In the ancient days, the historians used to write history centered around the kings and chieftains on the basis of this method. The traditional way of recording the life of the rulers and the way of life of the subjects in the olden states through personal study and enquiry was the mean of livelihood of the poets as well as part and parcel of their prime occupation. In this method the researcher or the investigator collects data through various sources about a person or the case under study. In this method the researcher or the investigator collects data through various sources about a person or the case under study. In the field of social sciences. Herbert Spencer was the first to use this method but it was later on in France that it came to be used as a scientific method for a study. Under certain circumstances and in particular cases where the emphasis of our study is on an in-depth understanding of the problem and the need for general solation is not great, the use of the qualitative method is indicated. In other words, if we wish to study a particular case intensively, we must use the qualitative methods because the qualitative techniques touch only those aspects of a case which are ion common with the others and, therefore, generalisable. In all the depth studies of singular cases, the case history method is used. The case study method is based upon personal study in which an individual, group, institution or phenomenon is recognised as a unit of study and various aspects of the unit are studied deeply. The study is carried out both with reference to past and present. This is what Good Hatt have said: "It is a way for of organizing social data so as to preserve the unitary character of the social object being studied." According to Shaw and Clifford, "The case study method emphasises the total situation or combination of factors, the description of the process or consequences of events in which behaviour occurs, the study of individual behaviour in its total setting and the analysis and comparison of cases leading to formulation of hypothesis." Bisang and Bisang say, "The case study is a form of qualitative analysis involving the very careful observation of a person's situation or institutions."

According to Shino Young. "The case study may be defined as a small inclusive and intensive study of an individual in which investigator brings to bear his skills and methods."

Ruth Strong has defined the case study as, 'The case history or study is a synthesis and interpretation about a person and his relationship to his environment collected by means of many techniques."

Giddings says, "The case under investigation may be one human individual only, or only, or only an episode in his life or it might conceivably be a nation or an epoch of history."

According to P.V. Young, "A comprehensive study of a social unit—be that unit a person, a group, a social institution, a district, or a community—is called a case study."

The case study method studies some subject matter which forms a cohesive whole and may be treated as a unit. It is not necessary that this unit must always be a person, it can be an institution or a group or even a community, provided these are cohesive and homogeneous. The quantitative methods study only those aspects of a subject which it shares in common with other similar subjects.

Therefore, they study a subject in its particular aspect and not in its entirety. But the case study method, on the contrary, deals with every aspect of the subject and studies it both intensively and extensively. That is, each element is studied deeply and no element is left untouched.

It goes without saying that an investigator may specifically analyse a particular person, place or thing for bettering the existing knowledge of the same. The case study method deals with both the what and why of the subject, that is, it aims at describing the complete behavioural pattern of a unit and having done this, tries to discover the factors which will rationally account for them.

In short, the case study method aims at description as well as explanation of the unit in studies. It also explains the place and role of a unit in its surrounding social milieu. The case study method also tries to perceive the unitary forces of the subject matter and organises it into an integral whole. A researcher undertaking this method may very well integrate and put together the wholeness of the materials regarding the subject-area chosen.

In other words, it is a view point which sees the social phenomenon as an integral unit. Accordingly, this method treats man, family, institution or group as a whole. An investigator who pursues the case study method may try to maximise the qualitative and quantitative informations from his inquiry by making use of certain procedures which serve him as aids. It is quite clear that the primary need in this method is to know the manner and technique by which the subject matter appears as an integral whole. The investigator must strive to make extensive collection of relevant materials which facilitate an overall view of the problem. The sole means of achieving success in the case study method is to collect materials about each of the aspects in a unit.

For example, while studying a person, the information about his social status and situation is primary but equally important is to gather all information regarding his biological, economic, political, psychological and philosophical aspects, including the religious, ethical and spiritual. Only then can we understand the unity of a human being and study him as an expression of that fundamental unity. The investigator has to bear in mind the fact that the entire data about a unit should be divided into suitable, separate and specific classes so as to synthesize the results and to arrive at categorical findings. Above all, a case study should be dynamic in its approach and operation.

It is not enough if it merely attends to the present structure of a unit. Therefore, the case study must range over the past, present and future. Moreover, the case study must be analysed both horizontally and longitudinally that is, we have to study it in breadth as well as in depth.

Survey Method

Modern society is beset with so many problems and every department clamours for solutions, rectifications and reformation. Sufficient information and necessary details about these problems may not be available in records, files and other sources in the concerned areas or departments. Hence, a study of these problems requires systematic gathering of data from the population by applying personal contact, interviews or other techniques. These are generally known as social surveys. The social survey plays a predominant role in regulating the different aspects of the socio-economic sphere and in all other disciplines including physical education.

The social survey is an important tool or technique employed extensively in all social science disciplines to gather evidence relating to social problems. It is a process by which quantitative facts about a social phenomenon are collected to contribute to the solution of immediate problems. The survey approach is followed in studying local as well as state and national problems.

The survey method helps us to build a body of facts and figures which possess greater significance and may do a great deal to solve immediate problems including those in the realm of physical education. Survey research is that branch of social scientific investigation that studies large and small populations, by selecting and studying samples chosen from the population, to discover the relevant incidence, distribution and interrelation of sociological and psychological variables. Surveys covered by this definition are often called sample surveys, probably because survey research developed as a separate research activity along with the development and improvement of sampling procedures.

The definition also links population and sample. Survey research is interested in the current assessment of the characteristics of whole populations of the people. Sample surveys attempt to determine the incidence, distribution and interrelations among sociological and psychological variables. The nature of survey research as a social science is revealed by the nature of its variables which can be classified as sociological facts and opinion and attitudes. Sociological facts are attributes of individuals that spring from their membership in social groups. Psychological variables include opinions, attitudes and behaviour.

The survey researcher is not only interested in the sociological variables but is also primarily interested in what people think and what they do. Personal interviews, mailed questionnaires, panel and controlled observations are the usual methods of obtaining information. The survey research approach has contributed much to the methodology of the social sciences. Its most important contributions have been in the sphere of rigorous sampling procedures, in the overall design and implementation of the design of studies, in the unambiguous specification of the research problem and in the analysis of the data. Survey researchers use a flowchart which starts with the objectives of the survey, lists each step to be taken in the survey and ends with the final report. The term survey has been derived from veeir and sur which means over and see respectively.

Therefore, the work survey literally means seeing over a particular thing from a high place. But this term has come to acquire a specific connotation for social sciences and other sciences too. In natural sciences, this term, is generally used for measurement and in social sciences it connotes a technique of collection of data or information through interview, questionnaire, etc. Some scholars are of the view that the term survey can be used only when a direct contact is made between the investigator and the subject.

But in reality, it is not so. It includes the collection of data through any method such as interviews, questionnaires, library or books, etc. In the survey method, the data are not collected on the basis of the experiments carried out under the artificial and controlled conditions.

The researcher may in person go to the concerned field or area, collect data from hypotheses, draw conclusions and then test their veracity. It is true in very many cases, as C.A. Moser said: "The purpose of many surveys is simply to provide someone with an information.

That someone may be a government department or a private body wanting to certain information for effective operation. Carter V. Good says, Survey studies provide knowledge about the nature of objects, events and persons. The social survey is called, "A co-operative study of a current social problem, situation, or population within definite geographical limits, ordinarily with some concern for a constructive programme of social reform and amelioration. C.A. Moser stated, "Sociologists should look upon surveys as a way and a supremely useful one, of exploring the field of collecting data around, as well as directly on the subject of study, so that the problem is brought into focus and the points worth pursuing are suggested.

Thus, it is essentially a technique of gathering facts about a social problem of identifying the influence of certain social phenomena, and of finding out the causes and effect relationship. It is also concerned with specific persons, problem-situations, and conditions. A careful analysis of history will reveal that social surveys are practically as old as the human race itself because from time immemorial the surveying of the various aspects of the groups, society and kingdoms was very much in vogue for administration.

The ever-growing socio-economic and other problems in human society instigated the social scientists to engage in the study of those problems and to find the causes and to take remedial measures. A good number of economists, sociologists, anthropologists, social reformers and social scientists have conducted a number of different types of surveys either independently or in collaboration with governments or research institutions. Those include general, specific and census surveys. The social scientists have been attempting to use social survey technique to gather materials in a systematic way right from the ancient days. The survey method is generally undertaken in almost all branches of knowledge for the following definite purposes:

i) To investigate the present status of the various phenomena;

ii) To simplify a survey already undertaken;

iii) To find out the solution for unsolved problems;

iv) To arrive at better methods for efficient administration;

v) To obtain responses and reactions from large number of individuals; and

vi) To gather a relatively large number of cases at a particular time.

The survey method has its own credibility as a

research medium for it is more realistic than the experimental. Its basic and preliminary structure upon which the essential and reliable structure may be built, its echoing of the generalised voices of the individuals at large, its valid and accurate results and its interpretative facts and figures make it more so. Glady suggests the following steps in the survey method: studying the situation and problem; formulating purposes; considering the type, scope and nature, securing cooperation; selecting the participating personnel; finding sources of data; preparing the survey report; estimating the effectiveness. The methodology of the survey research involves various steps which may lead an investigator to unforeseen practical problems such as sampling, the validity of the instruments or techniques uses to gather data, the validity of the questionnaire and the reliability of the data gathered from the respondents, etc. The researcher should be alert and careful not to commit errors or blunders in the steps such as ascertaining the general objectives, specific objectives, sample, questionnaires, field work, processing and analysis of data and interpretation of the findings, to arrive at appreciable better findings.

The various types of survey and the different techniques used in survey have their respective significance and value. In general it may be said that the survey throws light on the various aspects of the social problems and helps in the understanding the causes of the problems and the mutual interplay of the causes. A general or widespread survey helps us to get over all idea of the multiple aspects of the problem ranging over a very wide field and this, in turn can indicate problems for specialised survey.

A specialised survey may be called a depth survey because it studies a particular problem in a limited range. The conclusions of a specialised survey are much more reliable than those of general or widespread surveys. Accordingly, the specialised survey is more important from the scientific point of view. The postal survey is less expensive than the personal survey but it is possible only when all the respondents are its expensiveness and the various types of lures and temptations to which a field worker is exposed. The value of a primary survey is directly dependent upon the technique use.

Hence, there is lack of comparative material which proves a stumbling block. However, the primary survey is highly important because through it a first hand attempt is made to gather well-organised information on a subject which proves to be a stepping stone for repetitive surveys. The census and income data can be kept reliable only through regular surveys. Survey research has a wide scope.

A great deal of information can be obtained from a large population. While surveys tend to be more expensive than laboratory and field experiments and field studies for the amount and quality of information they yield, they are economical. Survey research information is accurate within the sampling error ranges as in the case of sporting activities. However, there are a few inevitable disadvantages of survey research;

1) survey information ordinarily does not penetrate very deep below..............

2) it is demanding of time and money;

3) any research that uses sampling is naturally subject to sampling error;

4) the potential rather than actual weakness of this method is that the survey interview can temporarily leave the respondent out of his own social context which may make the results of the survey invalid; and

5) survey research requires a good deal of research knowledge and sophistication. The competent survey investigator must know sampling, questions and schedule construction, interviewing, the analysis of data and other technical aspects of the survey.

The sources of Information in the Case Study Method

It well known that every form of research work calls for the collection of relevant data which depends on certain sources. The sources in case study are; personal documents; life history; additional sources.

1. Personal documents

These documents particularly relate to personal life. Their study is important from various angles particularly the episode connected with the life of the individuals, their place, concept, attitude, experience and the circumstances of those happenings, etc. Letters and personal documents may also throw ample light on the life, particularly the personal life, of the individuals.

The personal documents are very helpful in the study of the mental make-up and psychological studies of the individual. From the point of view of sociology they help to study the social relationship and the factors for determining and governing the social relationship. In other words, through personal documents, it is possible to know the secrets, the way of life, the objects and other aspects of life of an individual and to determine his behaviour. The case study approach has been successfully employed in developmental physical education classes especially for those students who do not improve through physical exercise.

2. *Life History*

This is an objective study in which various events of the respondent's life are studied with an attempt to find their significance for the society. It is not a pure historical narrative but more than that. In a historical narrative only events are narrated but in this method the motivating factors and the significance of the events in relevance to society is studied. The data in this regard are collected through many interviews, with the respondent and with persons intimately connected with the respondents. In the life history, normally two forms are made use of; firstly, the use of recorded material about the respondent and secondly, collection of data through interviews. In this type of study the entire life of the respondent right from infancy to old age is made subject of study.

3. *Additional Sources and Other Sources*

Apart from the two sources cited above, there are other sources which help in case study method. The said two sources do have a direct bearing on the study but the additional sources that have been enumerated help a study in an indirect manner. This includes books, magazines; literature and previous studies; government documents and communications. The case study approach has been successfully employed to explore the personal problems, prospectus, privileges, status, individual merits, talents and individual excellence in the field of physical education which in return can play an important role bettering the existing conditions.

The close study of a sportsman, coach and manager may positively cause new findings to emerge which may be useful to others to be come successful. The case study may contribute tremendously to the positive growth of a person or a branch of knowledge. A case study was conducted on Harry Crow Buck, "The Father of Physical Education in India". This case study includes a complete record of the personal and other contributions of Buck. These types of case studies are very useful and should be encouraged at the university level for a brighter future for physical education.

The Objectives of a Case Study

1. To conduct intensive studies of individuals within a defined group.

2. To attempt to generalise from a synthesis of the individual in the group

3. To contrast groups.

Interview

As the name itself suggests, the "Interview method" is based on interviews. It is a direct method or direct collection of data; through this method we can know the views and ideas of other persons and institutions. It is said that this technique rose with the rise of industrial society. In is said that this technique rose with the rise of industrial society. In other words, it may be said that it is the product of industrialisation. While on the one hand industrialisation brought collectivisation, on the other it made life very difficult and complex.

Personal relationships became difficult because of lack of contact with people. Through this method it is possible for a person to come into contact with others and know their views and ideas. It is a systematised method of mutual contact with people. It is rightly called a method of social interaction. The interview method is used very extensively ion every field of social research. In an interview, a social scientist or someone authorised by him for the purpose meets individuals to interrogate them about various things.

An interview is a direct method of enquiry. The purpose of the interview, however, is not to collect superficial details about the interviewee.

In an interview, rapport is established between the interviewer and the interviewee. Not only is the physical distance between them annihilated, the social and cultural barrier is also removed and a full flow of mutual ideas to and fro takes place. Both are trying their best to create their respective impressions upon each other. The interview brings them both on the same level and an emotional and intellectual contact marks off the method of interview from all other methods of social research. In the other methods, a formality and remoteness persist between the scientist and layman and this cloak of formalism never gets stripped in these methods with the result that the information and data obtained by the other methods can never have the seal of reliability characteristic of the interview. In interview, all formalities are laid down and the gate is opened for delving into the intellectual, emotional and subconscious strings of the interviewee. It is these sterling qualities of the interview which enable a psychoanalyst to unravel the depth of man and go to the very bottom of his emotional pool. Everyone has been an interviewer and an interviewee at some time or another and all have listened to interviews.

Some of these have been efficiently performed, while others have failed to elicit the desired information. A few have antagonised the interviewee, while others have cultivated a fast friendship. Some have been trivial in nature and others have been of great significance. It is common to feel, after such interviews, that something different should have been said or self congratulation follows some particularly shrewd question which cleared up an important ambiguity. Once in a while, also, it is recognised that the person who spoke with us felt a lot better for having talked about his troubles. Like other social activities, interviewing has many facets. There are many types of interviews and the purposes are also many.

Nevertheless, interviewing can be studied in order to develop the necessary skill. Although interviewing is easier for some than for others, everyone can improve his technique by learning to avoid certain types of errors, by developing an alertness to ambiguities and deceptions and by becoming aware of the purpose of the interview, as well as the interaction between interviewer and respondent. It is of particular importance that the modern social investigator develop his skill. Increasingly the social scientist has turned from book is to social phenomena in an effort to build the foundations of science. It is true, of course, that speech adds a further complex dimension to research which the physical scientist does not have to probe. The rock cannot speak but, as Max Wedcr once noted, this dimension is also a source of information. If it is not to be ignored, tools for its exploitation must be developed. One can maintain, of course, that every phase of any research is crucial. Errors at any stage may weaken or destroy the validity of the investigation. Yet the interview is, in a sense, the foundation upon which all other elements rest, for it is the data-gathering phase. Its importance is further seen in the gradual recognition, location and control of the interviewer's bias since the interviewer is really a tool or an instrument. One interviewer may not penetrate the mask of refusal which a potential respondent offers. Another will be given a cordial reception. One interviewer will meet cliched answers, moderate in tenor and logical in structure, from a certain respondent. Another may find that the same respondent is quite violent in his answers and due to his emotion pays little attention to logic.

These differences may be extreme cases but may still be encountered. Important differences between interviewers are generally found to be raising fundamental questions of interviewer reliability: "To what extent can the answers so obtained be repeated? The concept of the interview has become of greater importance in contemporary research because of the reassessment of the qualitative interview. Social scientists at the turn of the century used this type of interview almost exclusively. The interview was likely to be rather unstructured in character and more in the nature of a probing conversation. Guided by a shrewd, careful observer, this could be a powerful instrument for obtaining information. However, it was also an unstandardised instrument. The investigator could not offer definite proof that his data was as described. The interview was of the character of the anthropological interview, in which no other interviewer was expected to check on the information and the problem of reliability was not often raised. The development of highly structured schedules was seen as one possible solution to the problem of standard direction. Its most complete development, of course, is the polling interview, in which the same questions are asked of every respondent. They are to be asked in the same form, in the same order, with no deviation from respondent to respondent.

In this fashion, it is possible to obtain certain items of information for each respondent. This facilitates comparative analysis between individuals or subclasses. However, depth is usually sacrificed in order to gain this standardisation. As a consequence, there is a movement back to the qualitative interview through the use of the interview guide which requires certain items of information about each respondent, but allows the interviewer to rephrase the question in keeping with his understanding of the situation.

This permits the interviewer to express the question in such a fashion that the respondent can understand it most easily. Further, the interviewer may probe more deeply when the occasion demands. This permits a more adequate interpretation of the answers to each question. In addition, the development of content analysis and qualitative coding permits some standardisation of answers not of the yes no type. Thus, one of the basic objections to the qualitative interview has been partially removed. On the other hand, this method required an even higher level of interviewing quality.

The greater amount of the discretion allowed to the interviewer, the more necessary is a high level of competence. The application of more rigid sampling controls takes from the interviewer the choice of respondent. If, however, his interview report contains information quite different from the one obtained by other interviewers, the problem of sampling is raised–a sampling of the responses of the interviewee to these particular questions.

If the responses are entirely different from one interview to another, the adequacy of the data is always in question. Consequently, the development of interviewing skills as well as interviewer control to a high level is of great importance. The interview is a direct method of enquiry. It deals with the tendencies, sentiments and inner thoughts of a person who is called for interview. This is not suitable to physical sciences but more to social sciences. A social scientist or someone authorised by him meets the person called to question him about various things. In social life the interview is universally used for the study of human behaviour. The lawyer, the physician, the journalist, the social worker, the personnel officer, all depend partly on interviews to meet their professional demands. The social scientist also uses this method extensively in his research. Social scientists use various tools for the collection of data. The interview method is one of the traditional tools of data collection.

Much of the data in social sciences is generated by interview. The social scientists always have some sort of communication with people and derive insights from such communication.

Definitions

According to C.A. Moser, Formal interviewing in which set questions are asked and the answers are recorded in standardized form is certainly the norm in the large scale surveys. According to Vivien P. Palmer, "The interview constitutes a social situation between two persons, the psychological process involved requiring that both individuals mutually respond though the social research purpose of the interview calls for a varied response from the two parties concerned.

W.J. Goode and P.K. Hatt say, Interviewing is fundamentally a process of social interaction.

Young: The interview is a technique of field work which is used to watch the behaviour of an individual or individuals, to record statements to observe the concrete results of social or grouping interaction.

It is therefore a social process and usually involves interaction between two persons. According to M.N. Basu, An interview can be defined as a meeting of persons, face to face to face on some points. The interview or visit is a better method of obtaining survey information than the broad survey in which a mailed questionnaire is utilised.

The Major Objectives of an Interview

The aim of the interview may be usually finding out

views of others or finding the attitude of a group of persons. This objective may be studied under the following heads.

1. Collecting Information about Qualitative Facts

The social facts arc basically qualitative and are found in the form of ideas feelings, views, faith, convictions, etc. These social facts may be individual as well as collective. If they are dispersed in the whole society or group, they are called collective, or of the group, but if they are limited to an individual, they are called personal or individual. It is difficult to acquire qualitative facts easily and interview is the best method for acquiring these facts.

2. Collecting Information about Unknown Facts through Face to Face Contact

This is a direct method of collecting data in which the interviewer tries to collect unknown facts and ideas. This is direct method for knowing the ideas or inner feelings of other persons

3. Formulation of a Hypothesis

Through the interview we get an opportunity to formulate thesis. For formulation of a thesis, data or information about the problem is needed. Through the interview it is possible to acquire valuable information for formulation of a hypothesis.

Method of Observation or an Opportunity to Observe Things

Though the interview, the researcher of interviewer is able to observe things. When a researcher reaches a person to interview him/her it is not a mer interview;

an observer or interviewer observes events of the surroundings, the background and other things. Through all these baser variations he is able to make an assessment of the respondent and also his background. This type of observation adds to interview or an interview adds to observation. That is why an interview method dis-considered a very good method of research, particularly in sociology and anthropology.

5. Collecting Additional Information or Views of Different Person about Different Situations

It is a method for collecting additional information. We can collect information from normal respondents through schedules or questionnaires, but there are certain persons who suggest, or are capable of providing additional information which can be done only through the interview method. These individuals are aware of different social changes because of their intellectual status. They can be persuaded to give information through an interview only. The information so collected is known as additional informations.

Types of Interview

Interviews may be broadly classified as structured and uninstructed interviews.

The structured interviews are those in which a detailed pre-planned schedule is used and non-structured interviews are those with no predetermined questions but which proceed on the basis of only an interview guide. Non-structured interviews can again be divided into non-directive interviews, focused interviews, depth interviews, etc.

In non-directive interview, the interview the interviewer's function is just to encourage the respondent to talk freely about a given topic under a minimum of direct questioning or guidance. The interview method is significant in the purpose of measuring personality, and the services rendered by an association, a federation or a professional institution, collecting complete and authentic information and for acquiring information without exaggerations, distortions and inaccuracy.

There can be no doubt that the case studies so far conducted at the national or international level has contributed remarkably to bring out firsthand details about men and matters in every walk of life.

Characteristics of the Interview

1. The personal contact has the advantage out the informant by on-the-spot follow-up questions.

2. The interview may permit obtaining confidential information.

3. The interview permits the follow-up leads.

4. The interview permits the interpretation of the meaning of questions.

5. The interview survey would afford an opportunity for the interviewer to give information and to develop rapport with the respondent.

6. The investigator can form judgements of the adequacy of replies.

Framing of Effective Questions

The construction of questions should be simple and

short in respect of language. Complex questions that require the respondent to go through several steps of reasoning before answering are undesirable and have often resulted in misleading information. Questions on controversial issues should be broken down into components so that the tester can determine the respondent's feelings ab out many aspects of the problem, including those which he refuses to comment upon. A series of specific questions, sometimes refereed to as filter questions, is needed sometimes in order to gather adequately the reactions to all sides of the issue. The questions in the questionnaire should be arranged in proper order.

If the questions are not in proper order they may affect the response for which the respondent cannot be held responsible. The questions asked at the start of the interview should be such that they are easy to answer.

Such stage setting questions will help to build up rapport. They may be factual questions like name, age occupation or those which appeal to human interest such as fashion, film, etc. It should be ensured that such interest-catching questions are not sensitive and controversial. Advice seeking questions will also encourage the respondent. The questions should be arranged sequentially according to the subject matter or on the basis of period. Questions pertaining to one subject or one reference period should be grouped together in order to avoid mental exertion to the respondent.

The questions must be arranged logically and must move from one topic to another. The progression of questions should be natural and spontaneous. The transition from one topic to another must be easy and smooth. The transition from one topic to another must be easy and smooth. The questions should not jump abruptly from innocent to embarrassing subjects. While proceeding from one set of questions to another it is better to explain the break and the relevance of a new set of questions in one or two sentences. The questions which may embarrass the informant must be placed at the middle of the middle of the questionnaire, so that they do not sensitive questions, which may lead to the termination of the interview owing to the respondent's refusal to continue the interview, should be placed at the end rather than in the beginning.

If any such refusal is met, the loss of information will be relatively small. The researcher should, in all seriousness, take the utmost care before sending the questionnaire by prey testing it. He has to eliminate the errors in the framing of the questions, to remove the unwanted questions and to refine the language and the wordings.

Unwanted questions and to refine the language and the wordings. Lack of order in the questions may arise if the questions do not tap the same experience in each respondent.

This may be due to the use of difficult words, or questions which attempt to obtain too much data at one time or the other. Whatever the reason may be, totally unordered answers should always lead to a critical reexamination of the questions. The researcher should see to it that stereotyped responses such as the all or none responses must be avoided and such questions should be rearranged.

A high proportion of don't know or don't understand answers indicate that the questions are improperly drawn, or that a bad sample design has been used. A large percentage of don't know responses suggests that

a) the questions are vague;

b) they are too complex;

c) they involve difficult answers on which the respondent needs expert interviewing help; or

d) the respondent is simply not in a position to answer the questions.

During the course of the interview, some questions may be un-answered. The deerflies may be due to the inclusion of a taboo subject without any warning, or a question which is out of context. Refusal may take place if the interviewer asks personal questions in which the respondent thinks he cannot assure anonymity.

Suggestions to assist in the construction of the questionnaires:

1. The investigator should outline the field of study.

2. The purpose of the survey should be clearly identified.

3. The questions should be arranged in logical order.

4. The questions should be stated in a manner that elicits short answers.

5. Each question in the survey must be absolutely clear.

6. Pictures or diagrams in thew questionnaire may prove helpful in clarifying particular situations.

7. The investigator should remember the need for responses that can be easily and completely summarised.

Questionnaires

The terms schedules and questionnaires are used synonymously by most of the researchers. There is a very thin line of distinction between these terms. The schedules are used in personal interviews whereas questionnaires are distributed through other means.

The distinction does not seem to have a significant bearing on the principle method and important considerations in preparing research tools. The questionnaire is used as a tool in gathering a variety of data, such as the collection of personal preferences, social attitudes, beliefs, opinions, behaviour patterns, group practices and habits, etc.

The increasing use of questionnaires is probably due to increased emphasis by social scientists on quantitative measurement of internally accumulated data. The questionnaire like the schedule is designed to collect data from large, diverse, and widely scattered groups of people.

The questionnaire is generally sent through by mail, without further assistance from the sender. The schedule on the other hand, is generally filled out by the research worker or the enumerator, who can interpret the questions when necessary.

A questionnaire is described as a formal list, a catalogue of inventory and a counting device which is used in formal and standardized inquiries, the sole purpose of which is aiding in the collection of quantitative cross-sectional data. The main difference between the schedule and the questionnaire is that the questionnaires are conducted for governmental agencies or for non-profit research organisations while the schedules are just the collection forms which have no research value in the practical sense.

But, outside the governmental agencies, it is not common to make such rigid distinctions but to refer to the particular types of forms according to the predominant technique used in obtaining the data for enumeration, i.e., observation schedules, interview schedules, rating schedules, document schedules. But it should not be assumed that these types are mutually exclusive.

The interview schedules, for example, may contain items which demand observation, and likewise for the other type. In day to day life, there is a vast variety of questionnaires which can be classified in various ways. Here we confine ourselves to the structured and unstructured questionnaires. The structured questionnaires are those which pose definite, concrete and preordained questions, that is, they are prepared in advance and not constructed on the spot during the questioning period. Additional questions may be used when the need arises to clarify vague or inadequate replies by informants or when more details are needed than those supplied by them. The form of the particular questions may require responses which are either closed or open. The closed-from questionnaires are used when categorised data is required. The open-end responses are free and spontaneous expressions on the part of the informant who is not limited in his replies to a particular question posed to him. The open-end responses are free and spontaneous expressions on the part of thc informant who is not limited in his replies to a particular question posed to him. The open-end responses are used chiefly for intensive studies of a limited number of cases or for preliminary exploration of new problems and situations. At times, the respondent is asked to write a descriptive essay and express his viewpoint, describe his relationship, attitudes, indicate his problems, and report on details and events, without restrictions imposed as in the case of closed questions. The structured questionnaires are used in a wide ranged of projects both to initiate a formal inquiry and also to supplement and chock data previously accumulated. These may pertain to studies of economic or social problems, measurement of opinion on public issues or events, studies of administrative policies and changes, studies on the cost of living, consumer expenditures, child welfare, public health and numerous other issues. It is true that the benefits derived from the open-end question are also its limitations. Since it is non restrictive, a wide range of answers are usually given, some articulate and some meaningless, with wide intermediate gradations of response.

Obviously non-directed responses pose some problems of classification and analysis. The open-end question has been employed successfully where the primary information to be developed is qualitative in nature. The important value of the open end question is its use as an exploratory tool before an opinion has been solidified or before the research objectives have been clearly defined.

The open-end question has been explored very effectively for determining motivation by several persons. Generally, the questions posed in this type of questionnaire are sufficiently definite for the responses to be quantified, although much qualitative information is also secured.

Both types of information secured may either constitute the basis for a case study or supplement case and statistical data. Pictures have been used in some studies solely for the purpose of promoting interest in answering the questions. Unstructured questionnaires, frequently referred to as interview guides, also aim at precision and contain different subject matter areas, the coverage of which is required during the interview.

The interviewer, however, is free, within limits, to arrange the form and timing of inquiries. Flexibility is the chief advantage of the unstructured questionnaire. It is designed to obtain viewpoints, opinions and attitudes, and to show relationships and interconnections between data which might escape notice under more mechanical types of interrogation. The object is to give the respondent maximum opportunity to reveal how he had arrived at or developed his world of experience.

No checklist with predetermined responses is provided. Rather, free responses are solicited. There are some forms of questions which call for definite and mental attitude, i.e., questions regarding group activities may assume this form: How would you describe the activities in which your group engages? Or How do you account for the activities of your group? This pattern of questions is used for intensive studies but generally for limited number of selected cases. It has been applied to studies of family group cohesiveness and studies of personal experiences, beliefs, and attitudes.

The chief advantage of unstructured questionnaires stems from the danger that non-additive and non-comparable data well be accumulated when no structuring is imposed. While preparing the questionnaire, the first important aspect to be remembered is to make it clear who is to answer the questions. It has been said that, No survey can be better than its questionnaires, which means that however efficient the design or the sampling of the study may be, the success of the survey depends largely on the quality of questionnaires.

According to Pattan Shetti, the principles of question making are:

a) Use simple and familiar language;

b) Be specific and explicit;

c) Make the questions concise;

d) Make the questions self-explanatory:

e) Avoid ambiguous questions;

f) Avoid vague questions;

g) Allow maximum alternatives;

h) Avoid presuming questions;

i) Avoid hypothetical questions;

The researcher who undertakes the questionnaire

method should bear in mind the prime importance of framing the questions in such a way that the respondent does not find any sort of difficulty or irritation while answering the questions.

As Moser stresses, "It is fair to say that question design is the survey directors most persistent headache particularly since it is so largely a matter of art rather than science. It is always advisable for the researcher to take into account the knowledge of the population, subject matter, common sense, past experience and pilot work. Very careful attention and experimentation are needed to produce effectively worded question.

The language should be concise and directed towards producing uniformity of understanding among the respondents. There are various steps in designing the questionnaire. The researcher has to define the problem to be tackled by the survey so as to decide on what question to ask. The temptation is always there to cover much and to ask everything that might turn out to be interesting.

This must be resisted. Lengthy and rambling questionnaires are as demoralising for the interviewer as for the respondent. The questionnaire should be no longer than is absolutely necessary for the purpose for which it is designed. The survey planning must rigorously examine every question and exclude any that are not strictly relevant to the objectives of the survey.

In this respect, the pilot survey is the most helpful tool. All the marginal question can be tested out and dummy tabulations made from the results. Questions are likely to prove to be of small importance in the final analysis can be spotted and those which turn out to be not worth asking be excluded. In setting the scope of the questionnaire, the questions should be practicable. This needs emphasis, even though no amount of textbook admonition can take the place of common sense.

It is not good asking a person's opinion about something that does not understand, about something he does not understand, about events too distant for him to remember accurately, about matters which although they concern him, he is unlikely to have accurate information about, or that are so personal or emotional that valid answers cannot be expected by formal direct questioning. At the planning stage, it is necessary to keep in mind the following steps.

The researcher must learn as much as possible about his subject matter before he begins to formulate the questions. The researcher should lay out tentatively the logical implications.

At this point, the researcher should consult colleagues to get their views on the problem. With the formulation of the list of areas and questions, the researcher should submit this list to experts both in the field of the problem and in related fields. With such consultations some changes occur;

1. the list of possible questions grows,

2. the number of areas which are of interest increases,

3. the number of areas which the research can cover must be decreased,

4. the ambiguities, biases, poor phrasing, etc., are corrected gradually, and

5. a closer logical relationship is developed between the parts of the schedule.

Any questionnaire must be limited in its length and scope. In general, in the absence of special motivations for the respondent, an interview should not extend much beyond half-an-hour and even this length is difficult to sustain without fatiguing the informant. Self-administering questionnaires should not usually require more than 30 minutes to complete and an even shorter period is desirable.

Lengthy questionnaires will affect the morale of the interviewer as well as the respondent. Hence in planning a questionnaire, a researcher must get through the subject he has chosen for research. Then he has to decide the areas to be covered by the study and must frame the objectives of the study. This alone will ensure the collection of adequate and relevant data.

Consultation with expert in the field will also will also help to prepare an ideal questionnaire.

After the planning is completed, major areas of the questionnaire must be arranged in order to ascertain unification of the areas of the questionnaire. Goode and Hatt say that such unification is necessary in order to make the respondent:

a. get drawn into the interview by awakening his interest,

b. easily brought along from items which are simple to answer to those which are complex.

c. not be affronted by an early and sudden request for personal information.

d. never be asked to give an answer which could be embarrassing without being given an opportunity to cxplain, and

e. be brought as smoothly as possible from one frame of reference to another rather than made to jump back and forth.

As for the introductory item of the questionnaire, it should catch the attention of the respondent and should not result in refusals. It is better to avoid controversial items at the beginning. Generally, questions are devised in such a way that they have the power to evoke interest and to involve the respondent in the interview without arousing a strong controversial response. Secondly simpler items should be introduced in the first and items which require thinking or scratching of the brain or crucial issues must come in the body of the questionnaire. Such questions should not be taken to the end since the interviewer might have got tired or he might have got interviewer fatigue.

Likewise, questions involving too much personal information of delicate nature should not be brought at the beginning. It is important that sources of embarrassment should be removed from the questionnaire. Questions which are too personal and controversial should be avoided as for as possible. With regard to the last aspect of moving smoothly from one item to the other, questions pertaining to the same age must be placed together so as to have subject sequence.

It will also aid the respondent to answer easily.

While preparing the questions for the questionnaire the respondent's knowledge of the subject, ability, willingness, etc., must be weighed properly. If we are preparing a questionnaire for educated people, we can ask questions with standards of rich content or what are known as loaded questions. On the other hand, if it is for the uneducated the subject content must be kept to the minimum. Moser opines that "The surveyor should aim to ask questions only from those likely to be able to answer them accurately.

It is always well to remember that most survey questions are addressed to a variety of people very differently qualified to answer them. So much for taking account of the *ability* of people to give accurate answers; quite as important is their *willingness* to do so. Except in rate surveys where people are compelled to give information, there is no formal reason why they must answer survey questions. They generally do so partly due to general helpfulness and partly to their liking to talk about themselves and their views, and in part to the nature of the questions themselves.

But willingness is no guarantee that the answers will be accurate. If information is sought on a personal subject about which people are reluctant to talk, the surveyor must adapt his interviewing approach accordingly and be prepared to go to some length to check on the accuracy of the response. The prime success of the questionnaire method of research lies in the ideal framing of the questions.

It is obvious that much careful attention and experimentation are needed to produce effectively worded questions. The language should be concise and directed towards producing uniformity of understanding among the respondents. As uniformity in answers is very important for the later stage of processing, the questions must be worded in simple language to convey the same meaning to all the respondents. An increasing number of studies arc being conducted for the advancement of precision in question wording. The researcher should take the utmost care in using the proper vocabulary in the questionnaire

It should be within the comprehension of the least intelligent of the group studied. The phrases and expressions known only in certain regions of the country should be avoided. A question should be as concise as possible. Long, involved sentences with conditional clauses require extended concentration on the part of the respondent.

Such questions confuse them and will condense the wide range of information in to a small schedule. Questions and statements of a leading character should be guarded against. According to moser, a leading question is one which by its contents, structure of working, leads the respondent in the direction of a certain answer. Rather than asking the respondent, "Do you read The Hindu daily?" He should be asked "What newspaper do you read?" The question should be made explicit so that the interviewer is able to get the kind of interpretation desired. For example: What kind of radio set do you own/" may mean anything: the model, type or brand. Make the question pin pointed and specific by giving different alternatives:

a) Transistor b) Table model
or a) single band b) 2 Band

c) 3 Band or
a) Philips b) Murphy
c) Bush d) Others

The question should be self explanatory as for as far as possible, so that the desired information is gathered and tabulation becomes easy. The questions must be made most explicit and specific. So also, units of enumeration such as rupees, praise, weights in terms of kegs, height and length in meters, the time taken for completing a race and the distance covered in various events should be clearly defined in the schedule. Questions having ambiguous meanings should be avoided at all costs.

Ambiguous questions will mean different things to different people. They are confusing and beyond the comprehension of respondents. For example, the question; "Have you paid back the loan you obtained from the Employers Association?" If asked irrespective of the fact whether one obtained the loan or not will be understood differently. A No for such question will either mean that one has not obtained a loan or one has not paid back the loan. When descriptive adjectives and adverbs like good, bad fair, or frequently, occasionally, rarely, are used, such words do not have any accepted or agreed meaning. Similarly phrases like kind of generally on the whole, etc., should be avoided.